SOUVENIR WEAPONS PLAQUES

of

MOROLAND MUSEUM

field guide

Fourth Edition

Volume #01

Written by
Author/Publisher
Bruce Jenkins

Graphic Artist
Jess Holloway

Photographer
Bruce Jenkins/Ben VerVer

WEAPON SOUVENIR PLAQUES OF MOROLAND MUSEUM by Bruce Jenkins

Books may be purchased in quantity and/or special sales by contacting Moroland Museum at:

www.morolandmuseum.com
morolandmuseum@gmail.com

Published by: Moroland Museum
Author & Photography by: Bruce Jenkins
Graphic Artist by: Jess Holloway

First Edition

Printed in USA

This book is dedicated to

the people of the Philippines, their weapons and artifacts,

our families and the to all our friends of Moroland.

God bless you all!

TABLE OF CONTENTS

INTRODUCTION

This book was created as a Historical Pictorial Publication for use by collectors and people wanting to have a reference guide for these plaques. These plaques typically show miniature replicas of the many types of weapons used by the Moro People of the Philippines. These plaques come in many different sizes, shapes and colors.

Although most of these plaques have the words *"WEAPONS OF MOROLAND"* painted on the top, a few of the older plaques have different phrases such as *"PHILIPPINES MORO WEAPONS"*, *"WEAPONS OF THE MOUNTAIN PROVIDENCE"*, *"WEAPONS OF MINDANAO"* or *"IGOROT WEAPONS"*.

This book represents a unique part of the Filipino history, starting from 1945 and going forward to the current *"WEAPONS OF MOROLAND "* plaques being sold in the vendors stalls on the streets of manila today.

Historical Moro Background:

The last campaign of the Philippine Insurrection of the early 20th century was the Moro Rebellion (1899–1913). It was an armed conflict between Moro revolutionary groups and the United States military. The US Army found the Moro's to be highly skilled and resourceful fighters with their many types of edged weapons. After the campaign was over, a great interest in Moro weapons arose which inspired the Filipino natives to create these plaques as tourist souvenirs to sell.

Hard to find:

The older "Weapons of Moroland" plaques are getting hard to find and even harder to find in good condition. The Vinta boat "Weapons of Moroland" plaques are difficult to find as well.

Military Personnel's influence on these plaques:

Although many tourist have brought these plaques home from the Philippines, the majority of these plaques were brought home by the Service men\women from the major wars (*WWII, Korea, Vietnam*) and while on deployment to or near the area during peaceful times. They were brought home as souvenirs from their foreign country travels to share with their families and friends.

Craftsmanship and Quality:

Most of the older plaques show a very high level of craftsmanship and quality. Although the newer plaques are still nice, they lack the detail and workmanship that make the older ones so unique. When you inspect the very old plaques, the detail put into each item is obvious as they are like masterpieces on which the craftsman shows off their talents. Some of the oldest and most valuable plaques are made of ebony, ivory, and silver.

SOUVENIR WEAPONS PLAQUES

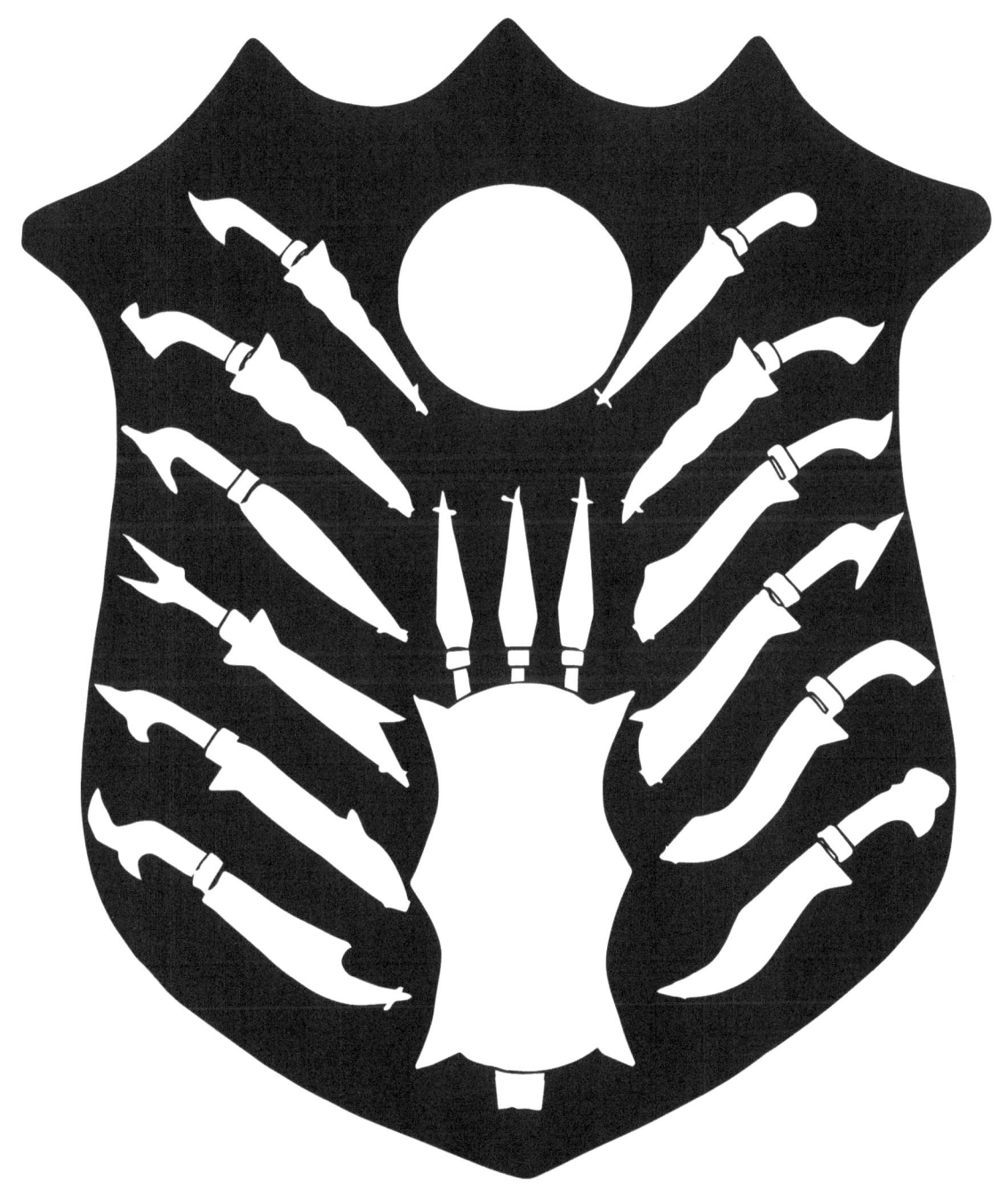

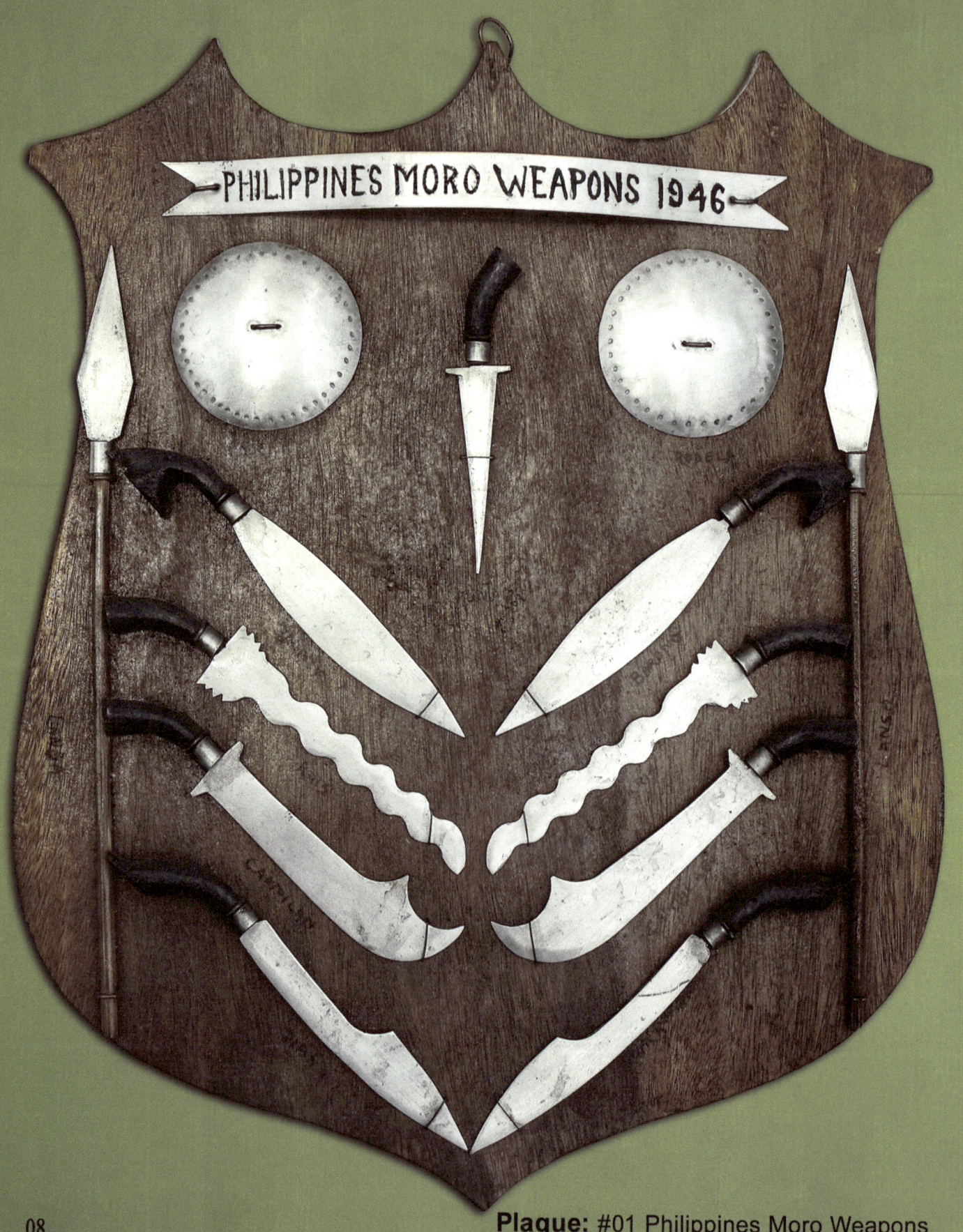

PHILIPPINES MORO WEAPONS 1946

Plaque: #01 Philippines Moro Weapons

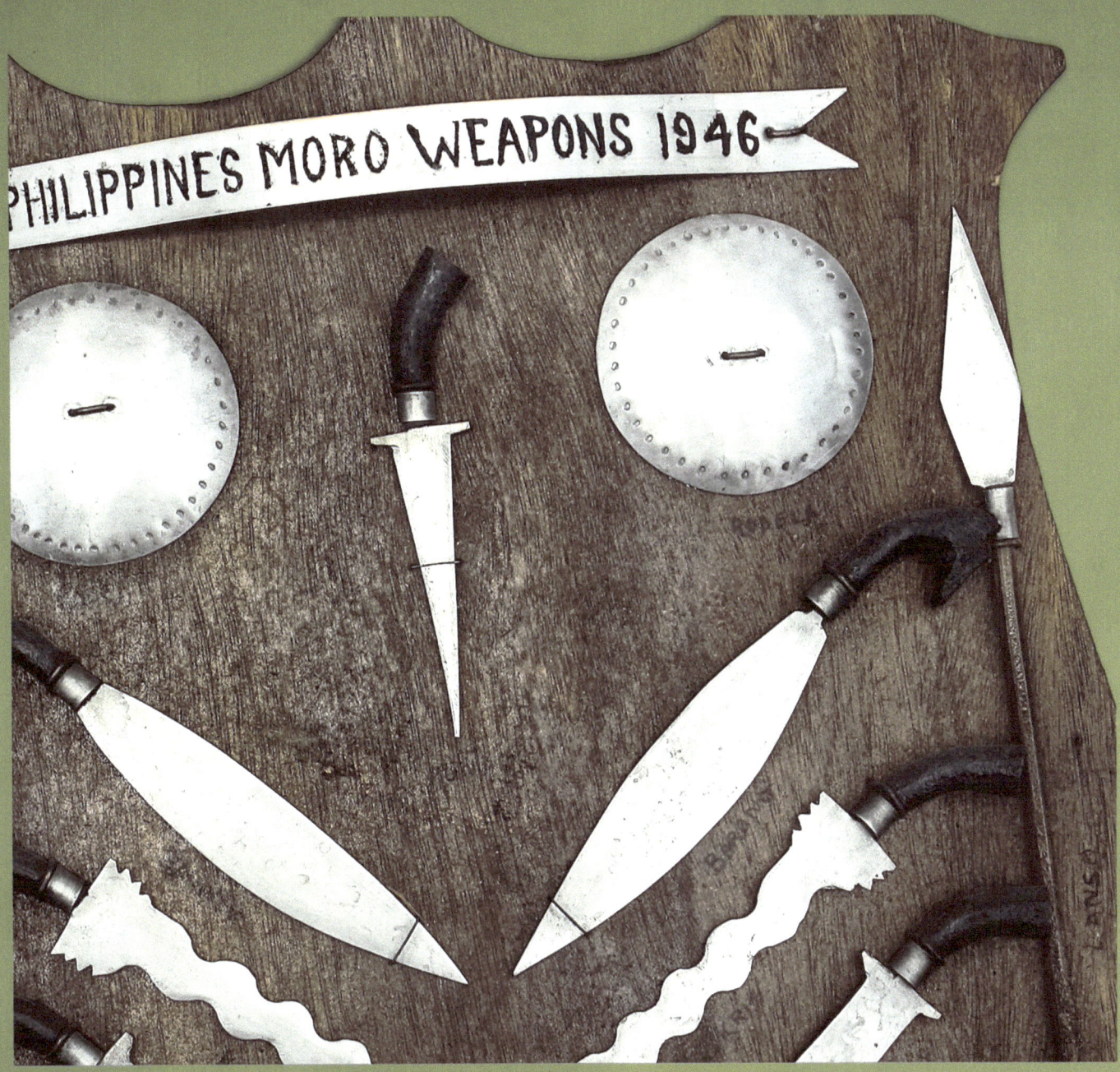

Plaque: #01 Philippines Moro Weapons

Description:

    This is an antique 1946 Philippines Moro weapons display. It has replica's of the weapons that were used by the Moro tribe during this time. A WWII veteran purchased this plaque while he was stationed in the Philippines.

Location Found:	Philippines	**Height:**	10.5 inches
Location Purchased:	EBay	**Width:**	8.5 inches
Approximate Age:	1946	**Condition:**	Average

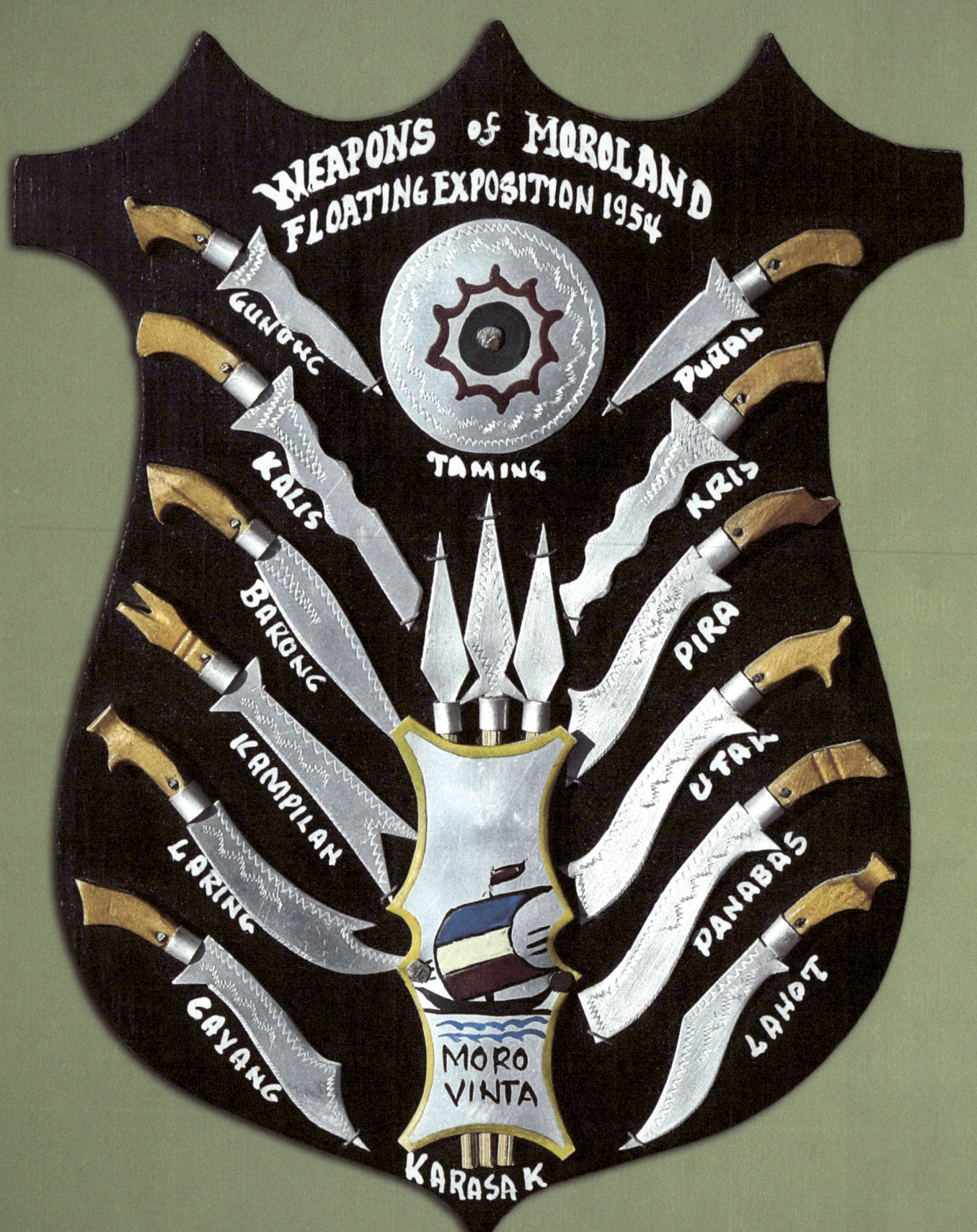

Plaque: #02 Philippines Moro Weapons

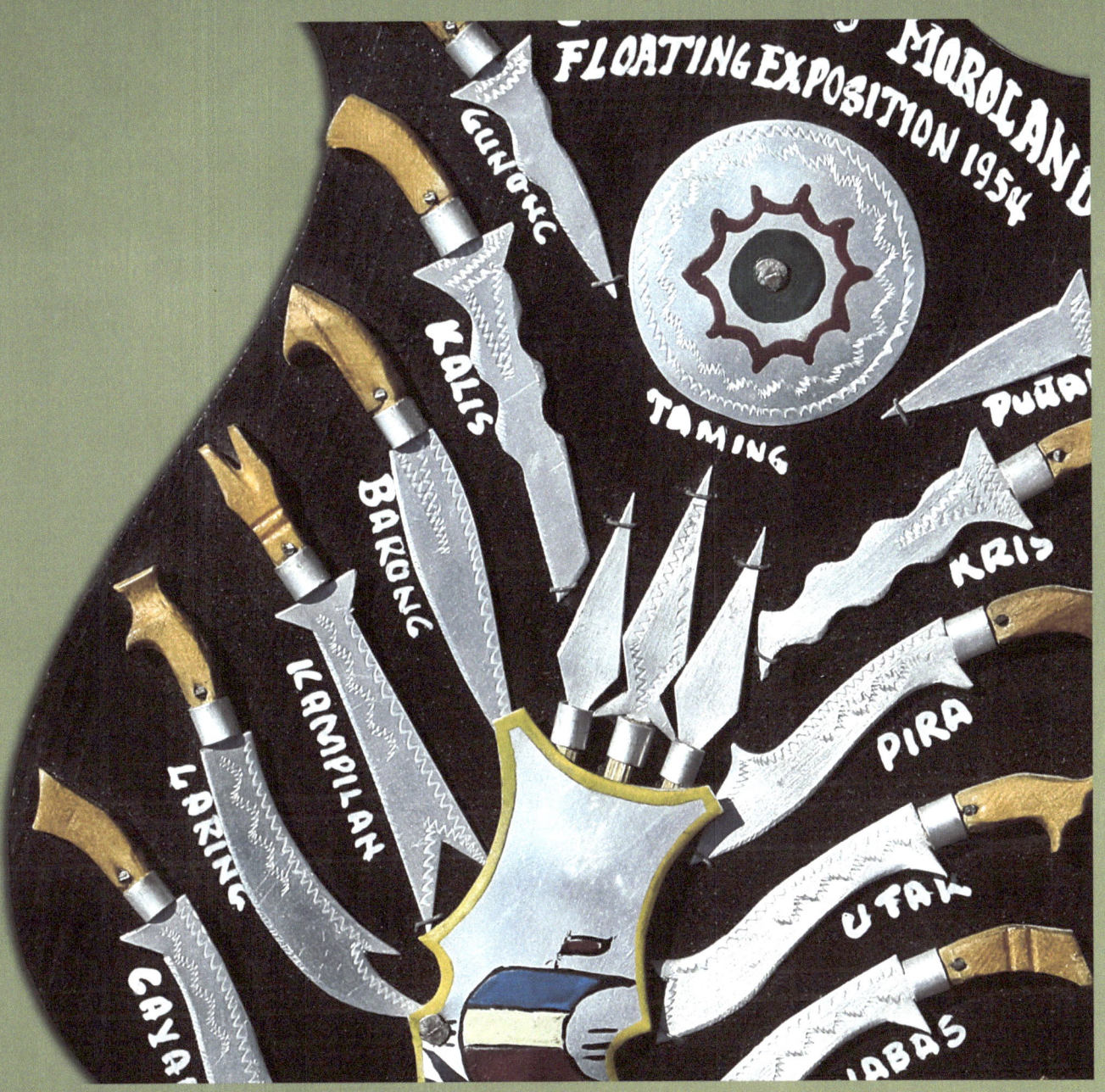

Plaque: #02 Philippines Moro Weapons

Description:

   This is a "Weapons of Moroland Floating Exposition 1954" Wall Plaque. It was brought back by a Korean War veteran. It has hand carved wooden handles with aluminum cut-out weapons.

Location Found:	Cebu, Philippines	**Height:**	6 inches
Location Purchased:	EBay	**Width:**	5 inches
Approximate Age:	1954	**Condition:**	Above Average

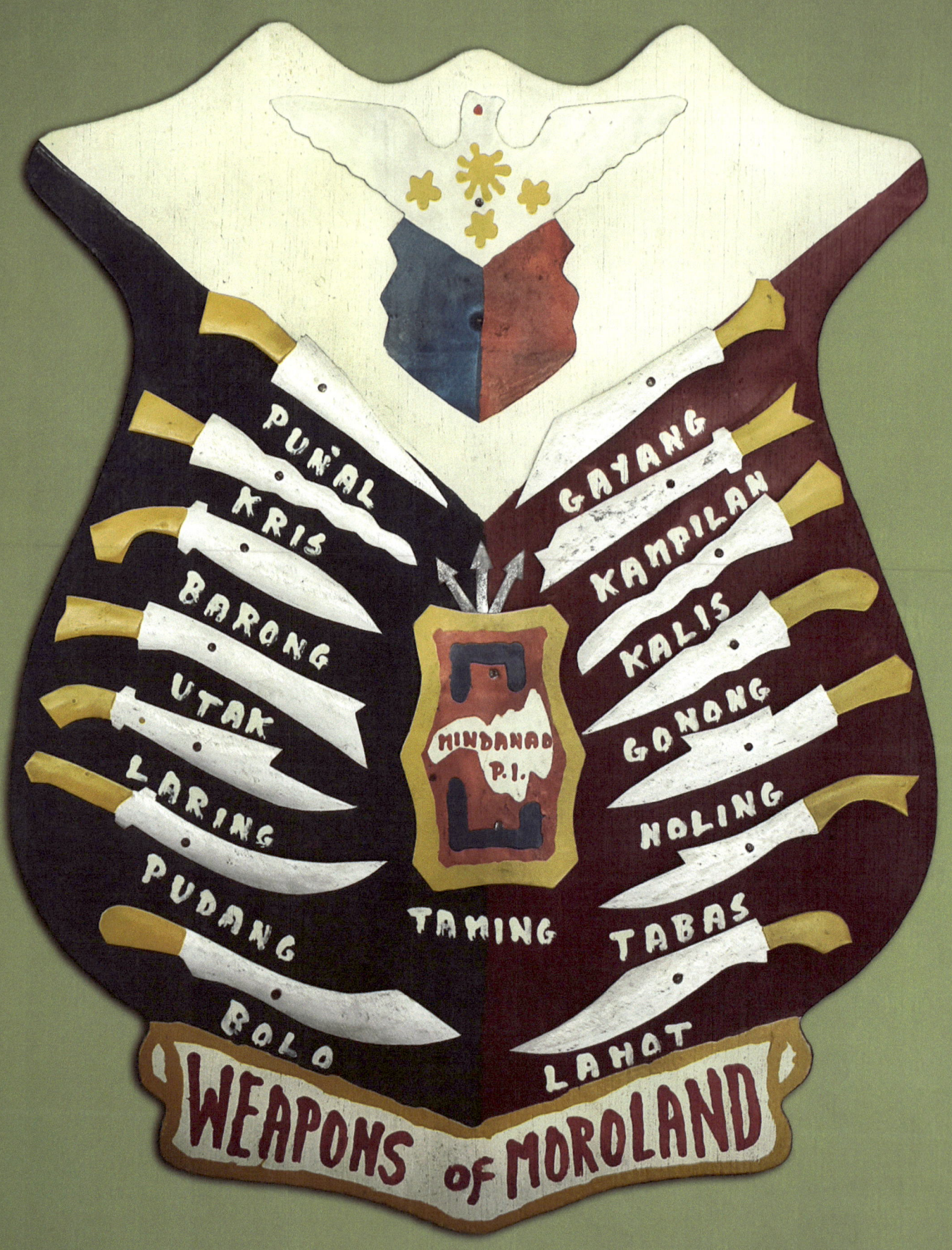

Plaque: #03 Philippines Moro Weapons

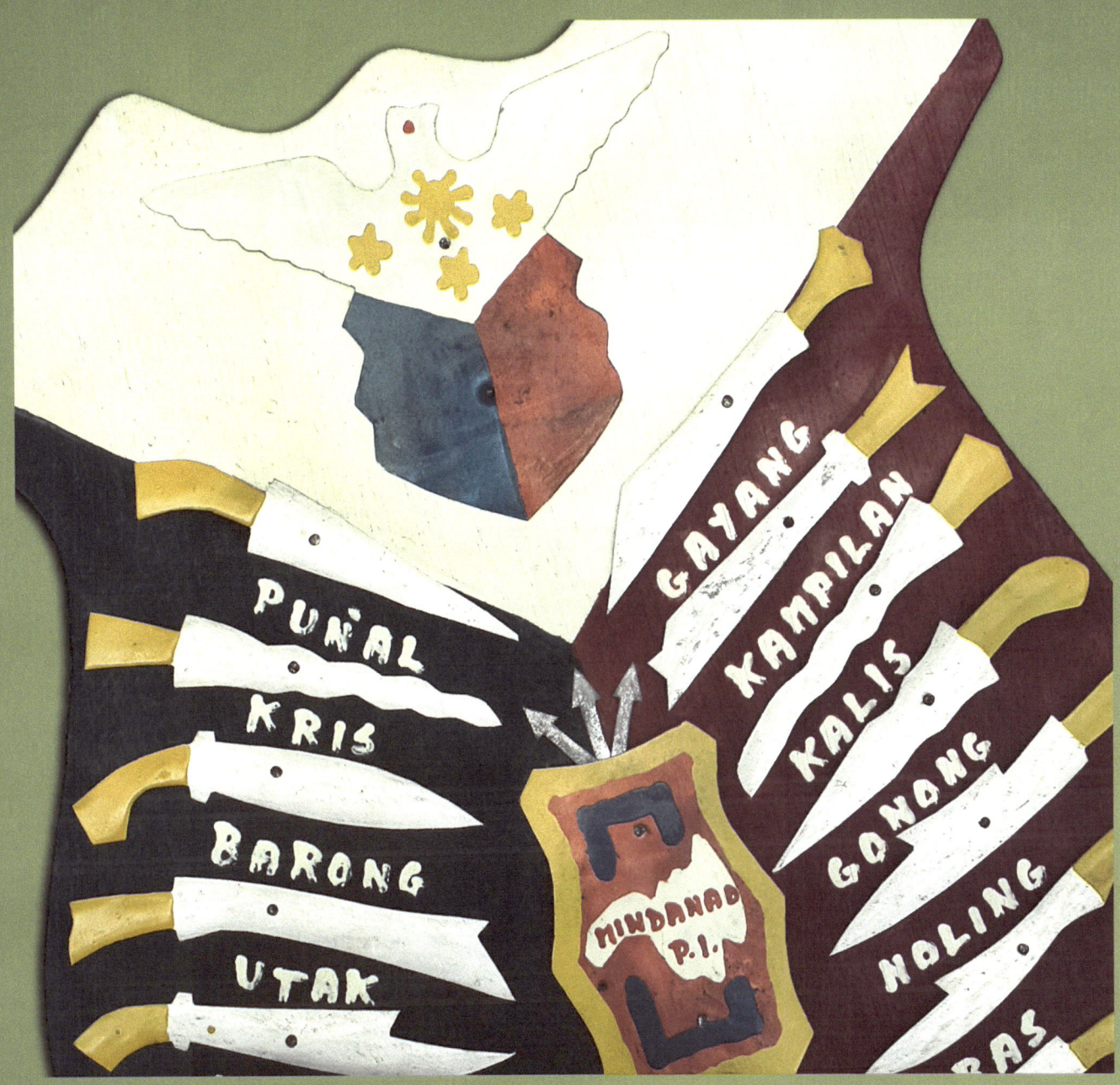

Plaque: #03 Philippines Moro Weapons

Description:

This is a vintage Weapons of Moroland travel souvenir plaque. It was made by native islanders and sold to tourists. It has 14 cut-tin knives, hand painted shield and eagle insignia.

Location Found:	Philippines	**Height:**	13 inches
Location Purchased:	EBay	**Width:**	10.25 inches
Approximate Age:	1950's	**Condition:**	Average

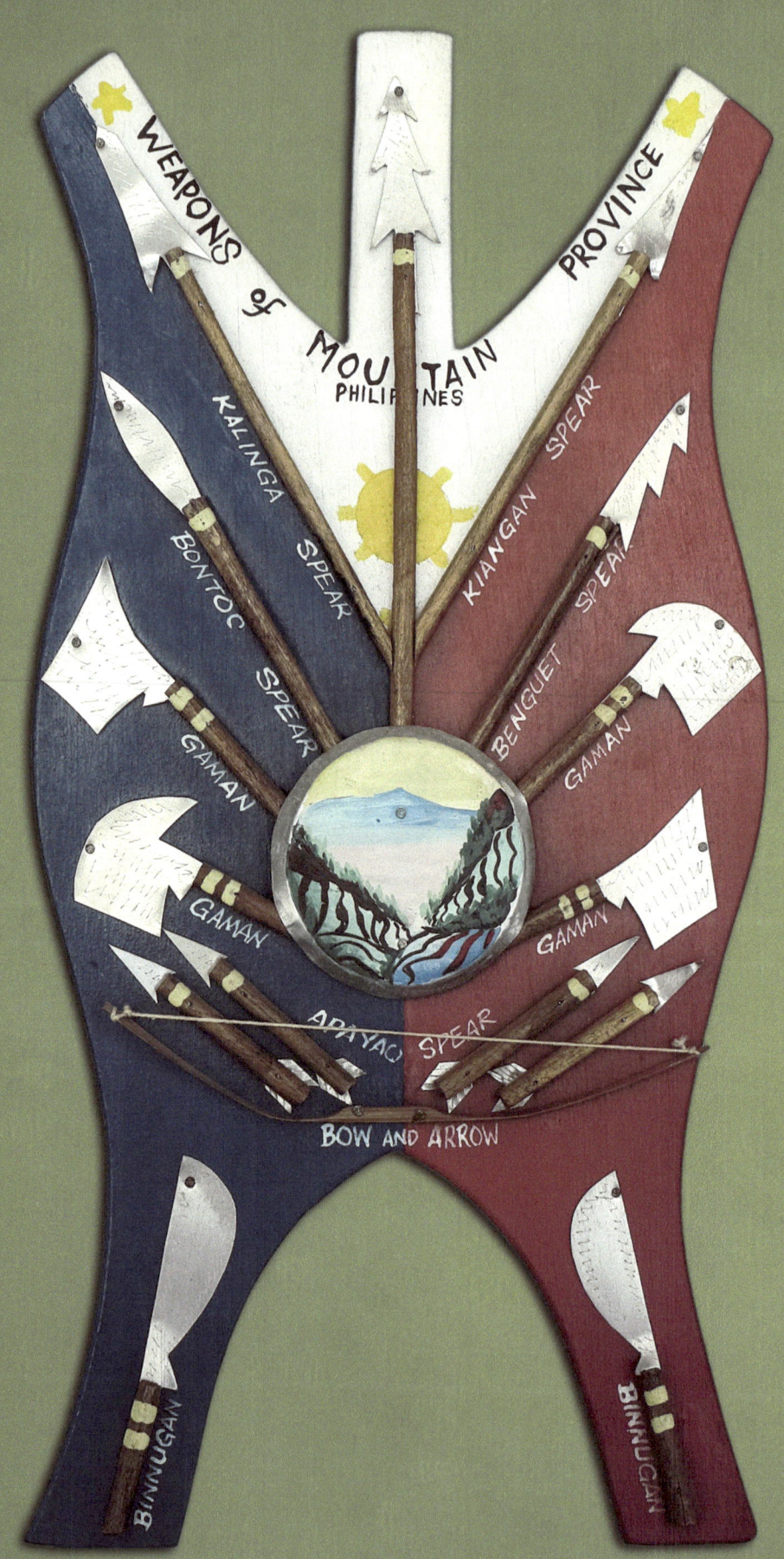

14

Plaque: #04 Philippines Moro Weapons

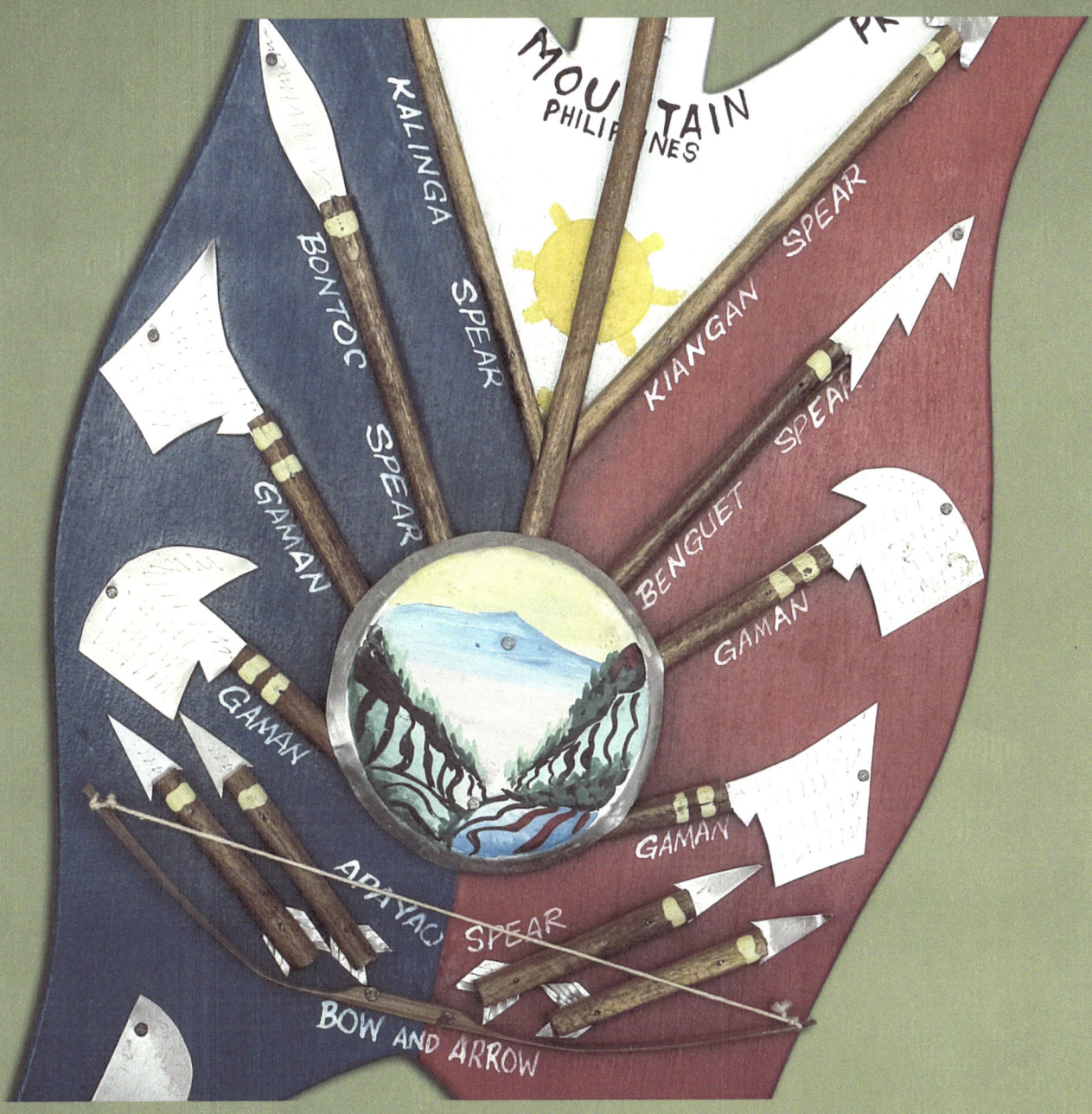

Plaque: #04 Philippines Moro Weapons

Description:

   This is a handmade souvenir weapons plaque from the Philippines. It has replicas of the different weapons used by the mountain people. There are 16 weapons represented on the plaque with their names under each one. The weapons range from 6" long to 2½" long and are made of wood and tin.

Location Found:	Philippines	**Height:**	14 inches
Location Purchased:	EBay	**Width:**	7 inches
Approximate Age:	1950's	**Condition:**	Above Average

15

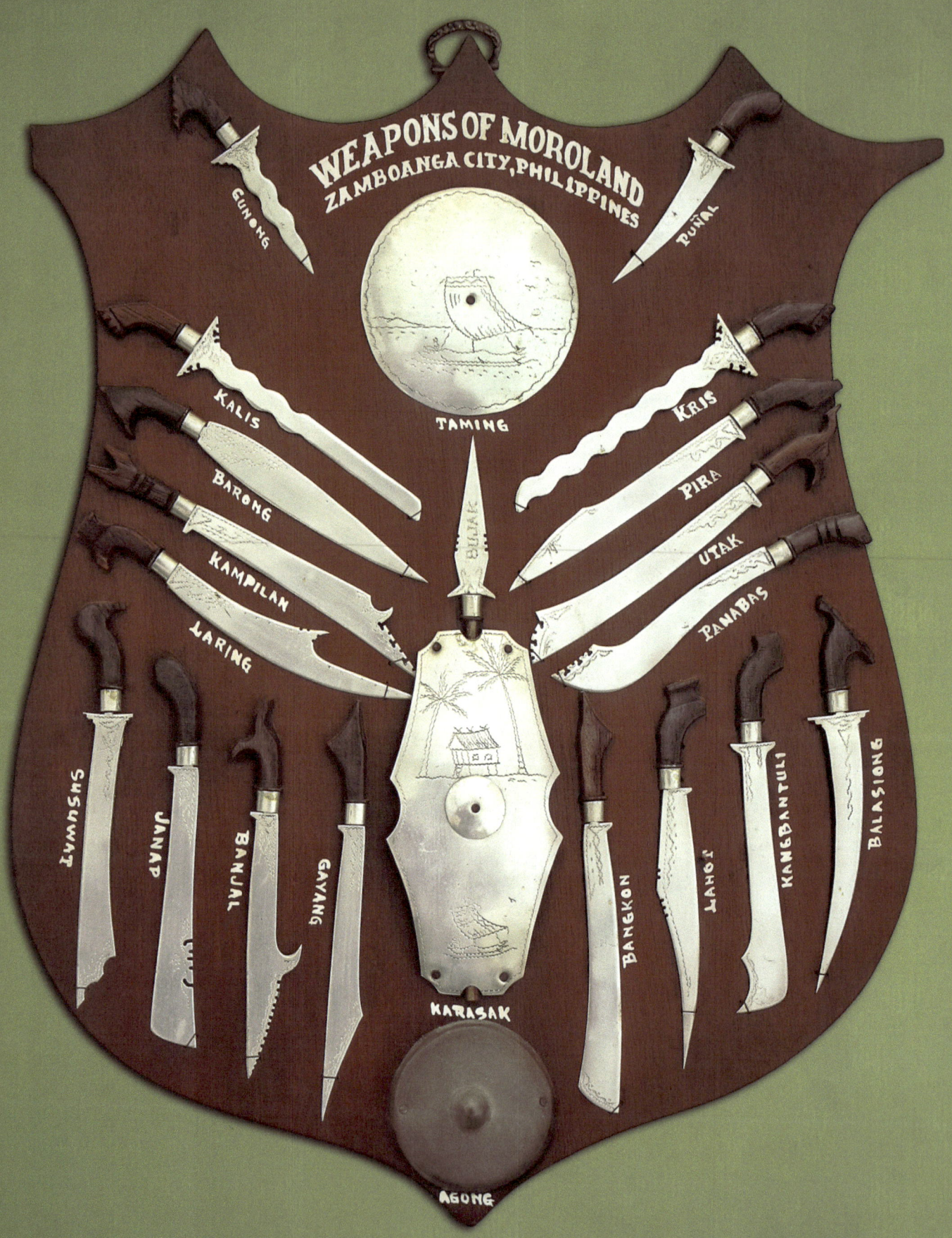

Plaque: #05 Philippines Moro Weapons

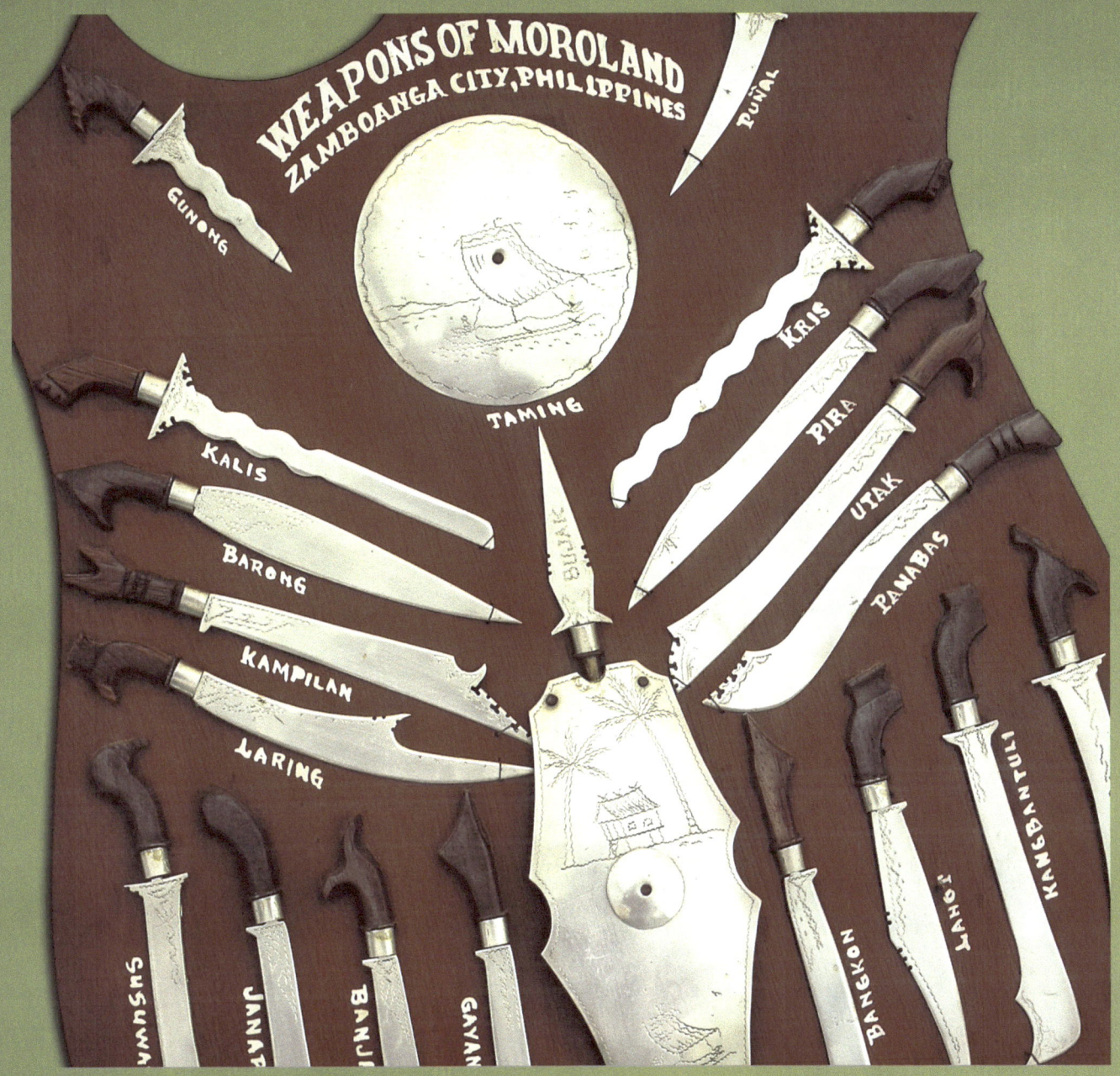

Plaque: #05 Philippines Moro Weapons

Description:
    This is a miniature Handcrafted Weapons of Moroland Plaque. This is a tourist souvenir made of wood and tin by the Filipino natives.

Location Found:	Zamboanga City, Philippines	**Height:**	14 inches
Location Purchased:	EBay	**Width:**	11.5 inches
Approximate Age:	1948 - 1950	**Condition:**	Museum Quality

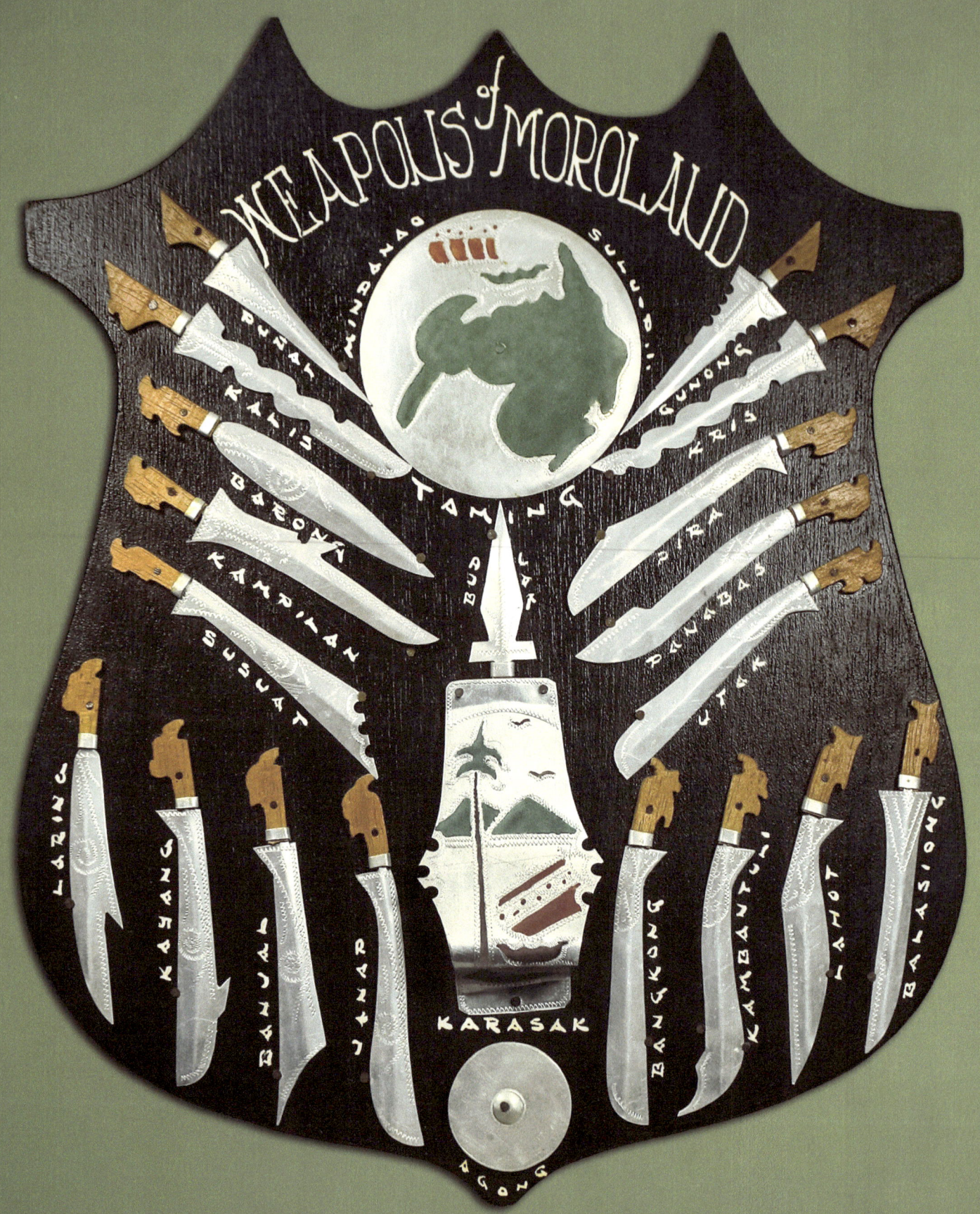

Plaque: #06 Philippines Moro Weapons

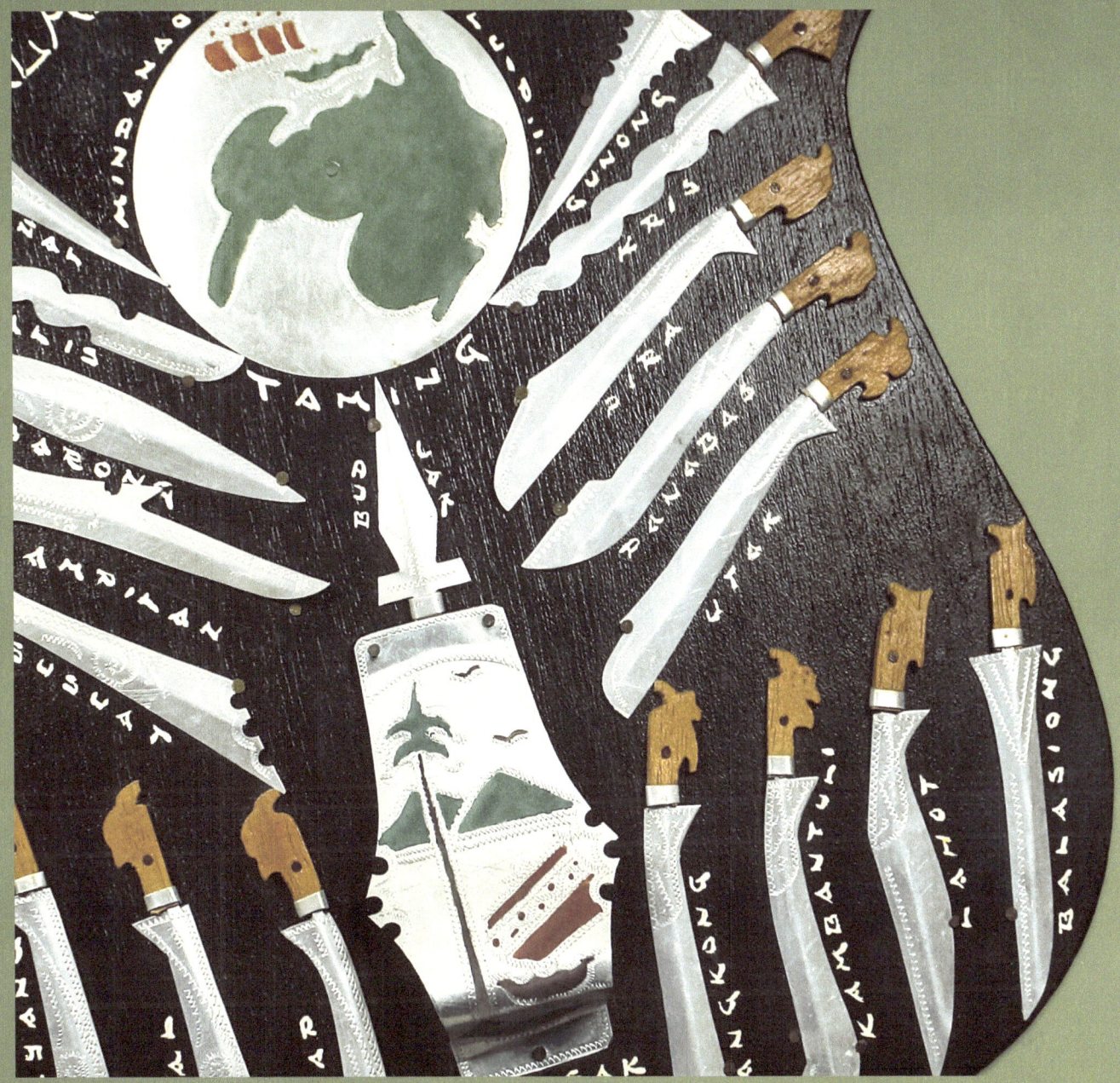

Plaque: #06 Philippines Moro Weapons

Description:

    This is a Weapons of Moroland plaque. It is a handcrafted tourist souvenir made of wood and aluminum by the Filipino natives.

Location Found:	Mindanao, Philippines	**Height:**	14 inches
Location Purchased:	EBay	**Width:**	11.5 inches
Approximate Age:	1960	**Condition:**	Above Average

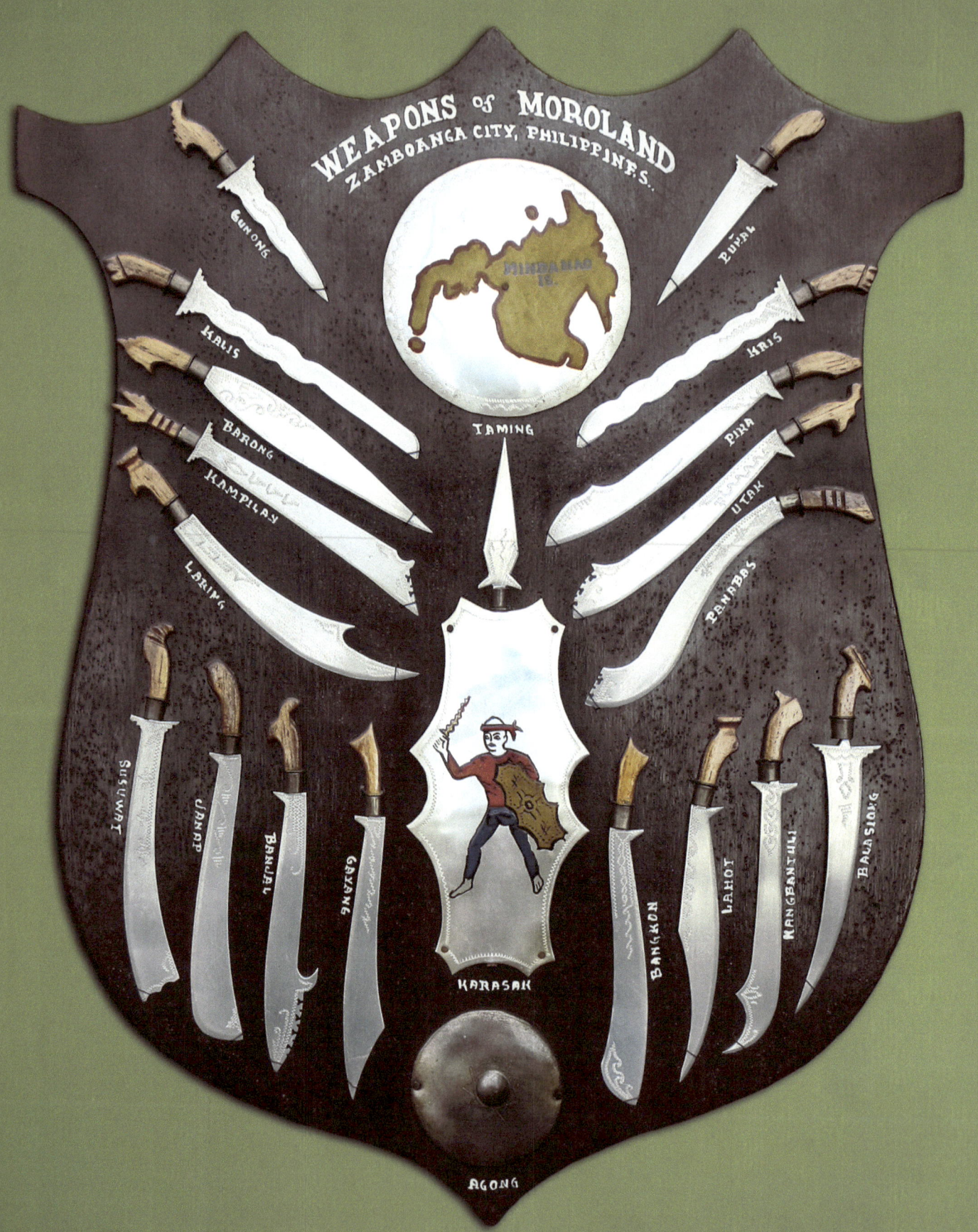

Plaque: #07 Philippines Moro Weapons

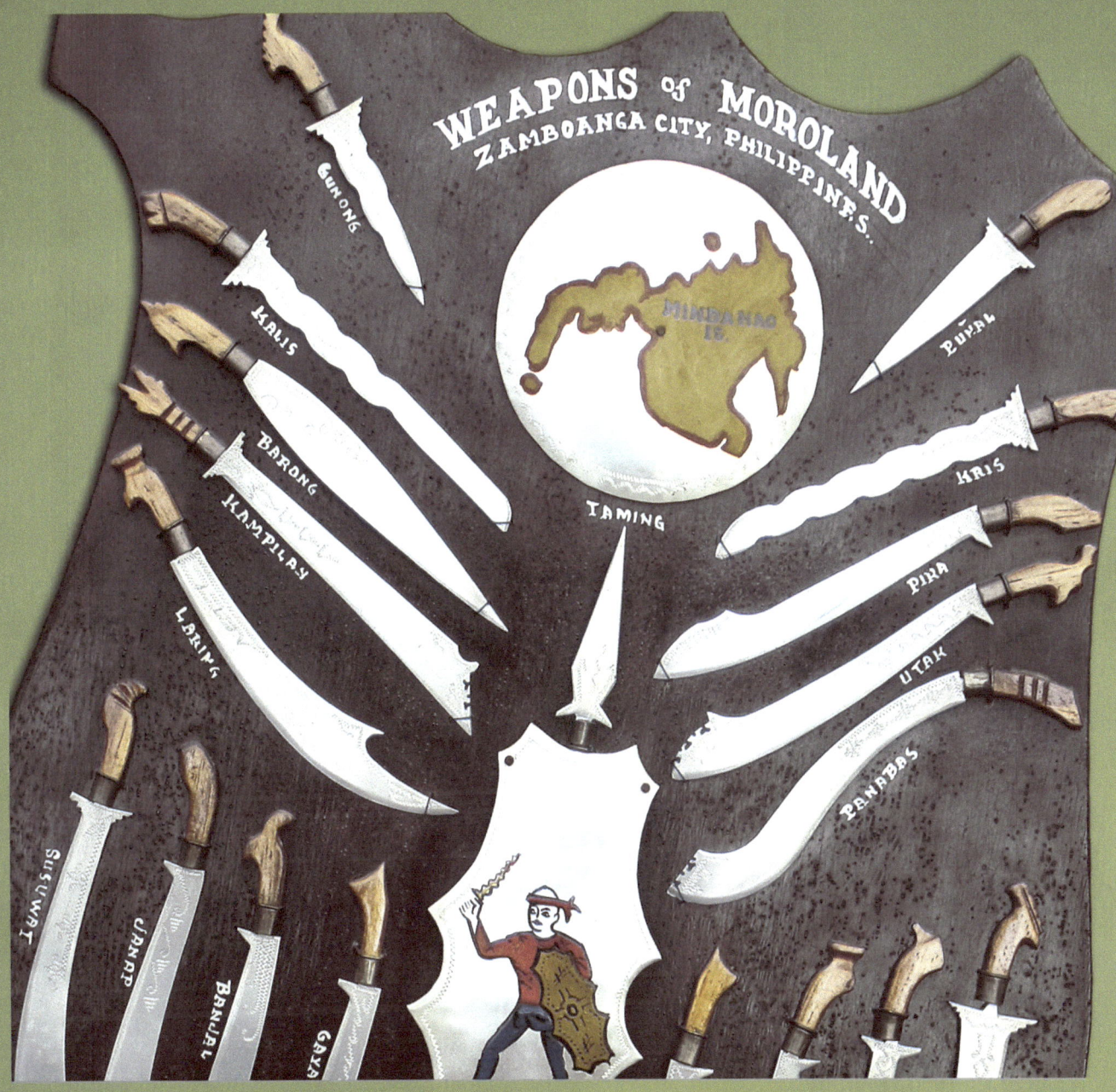

Plaque: #07 Philippines Moro Weapons

Description:
    This is a miniature handcrafted Weapons of Moroland Plaque. It is a tourist souvenir made of wood and aluminum by Filipino natives.

Location Found:	Mindanao, Philippines	**Height:**	14 inches
Location Purchased:	EBay	**Width:**	11.5 inches
Approximate Age:	1960's	**Condition:**	Above Average

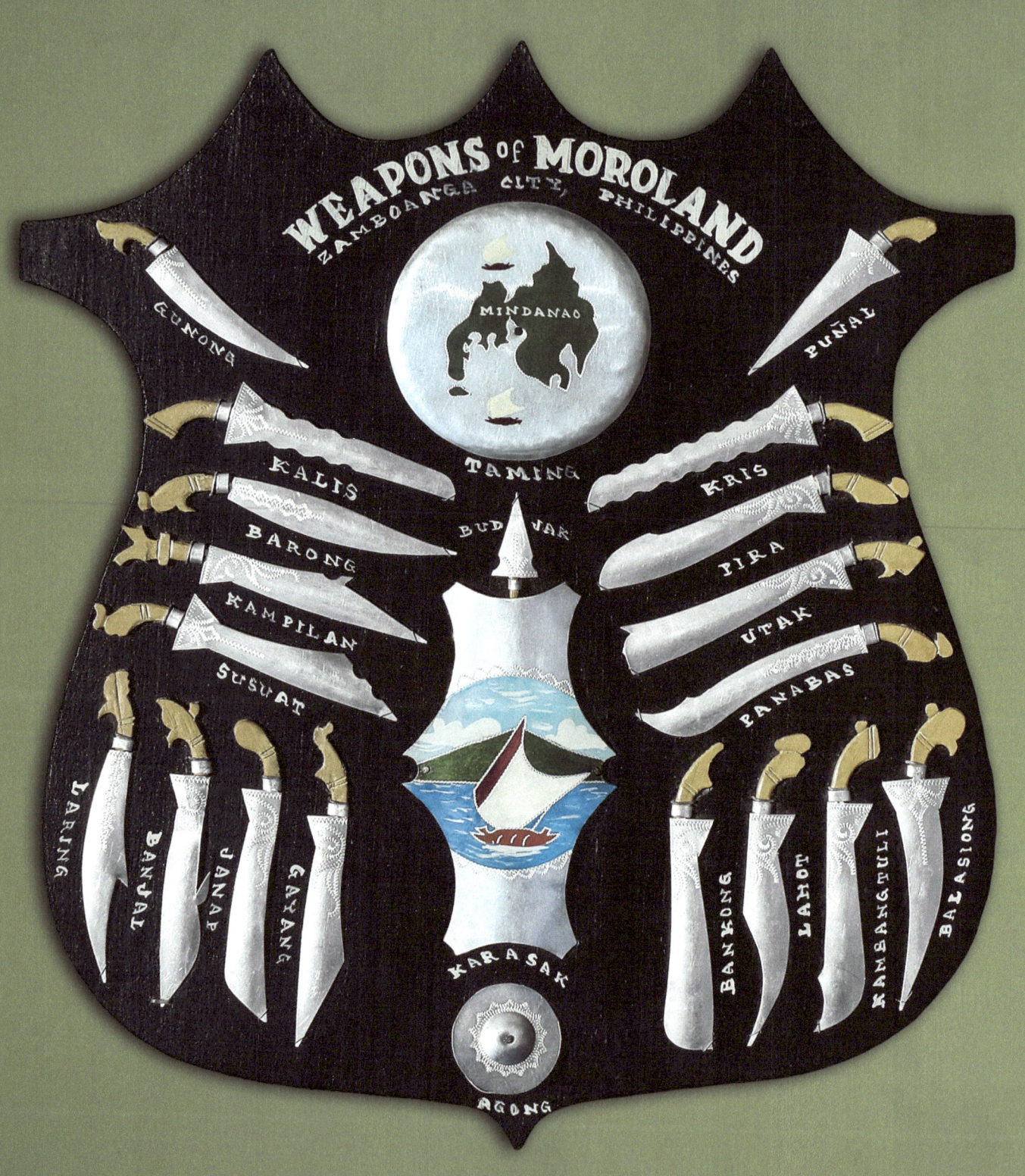

Plaque: #08 Philippines Moro Weapons

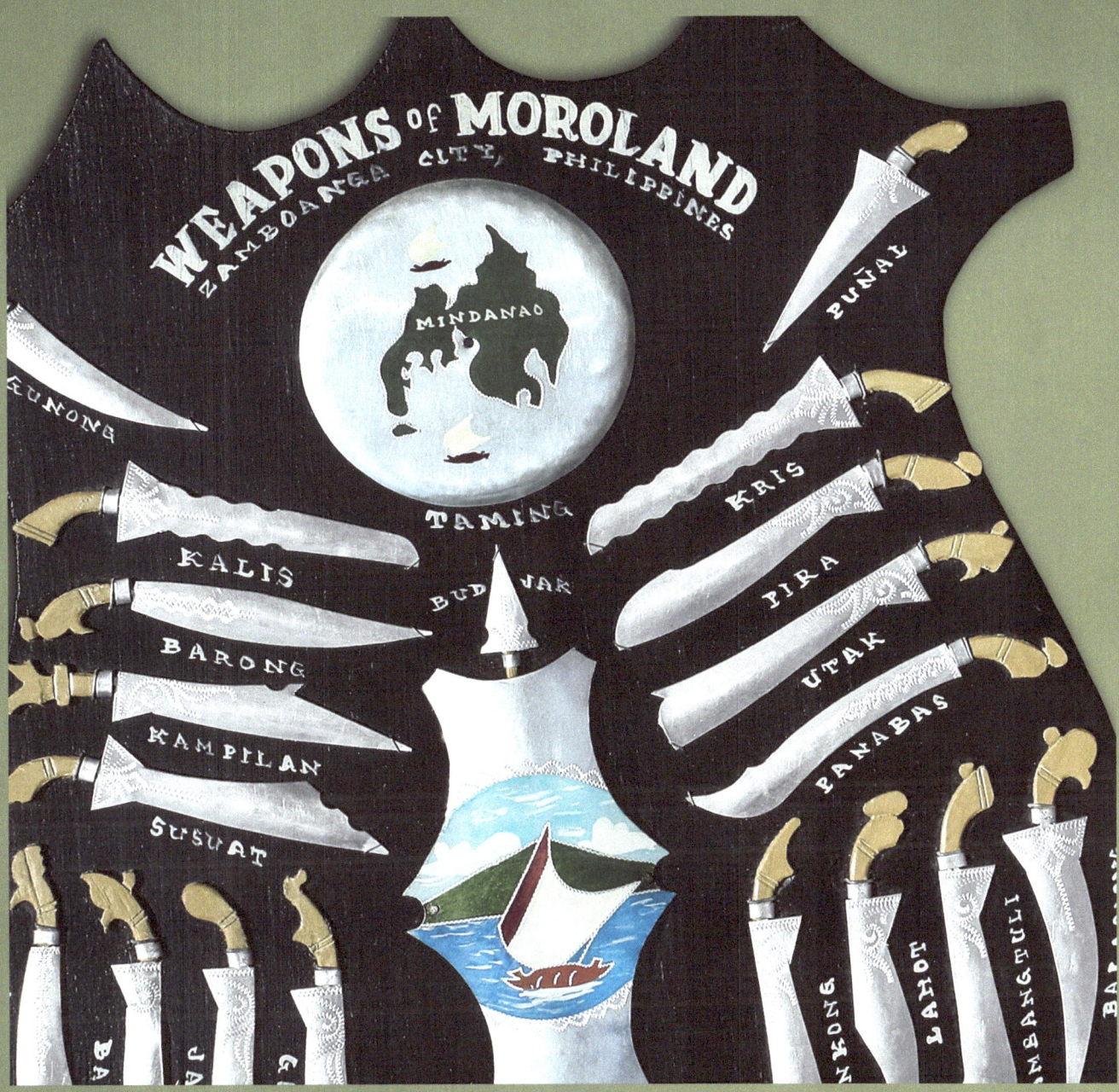

Plaque: #08 Philippines Moro Weapons

Description:

    Vintage hand made Weapons Of Moroland plaque shield. This wall display features 18 assorted swords, arrow and other weapons. This plaque was brought back from the southern Philippines by a Korean war veteran.

Location Found:	Zamboanga City, Philippines	**Height:**	13.25 inches
Location Purchased:	EBay	**Width:**	11.5 inches
Approximate Age:	1950's	**Condition:**	Museum Quality

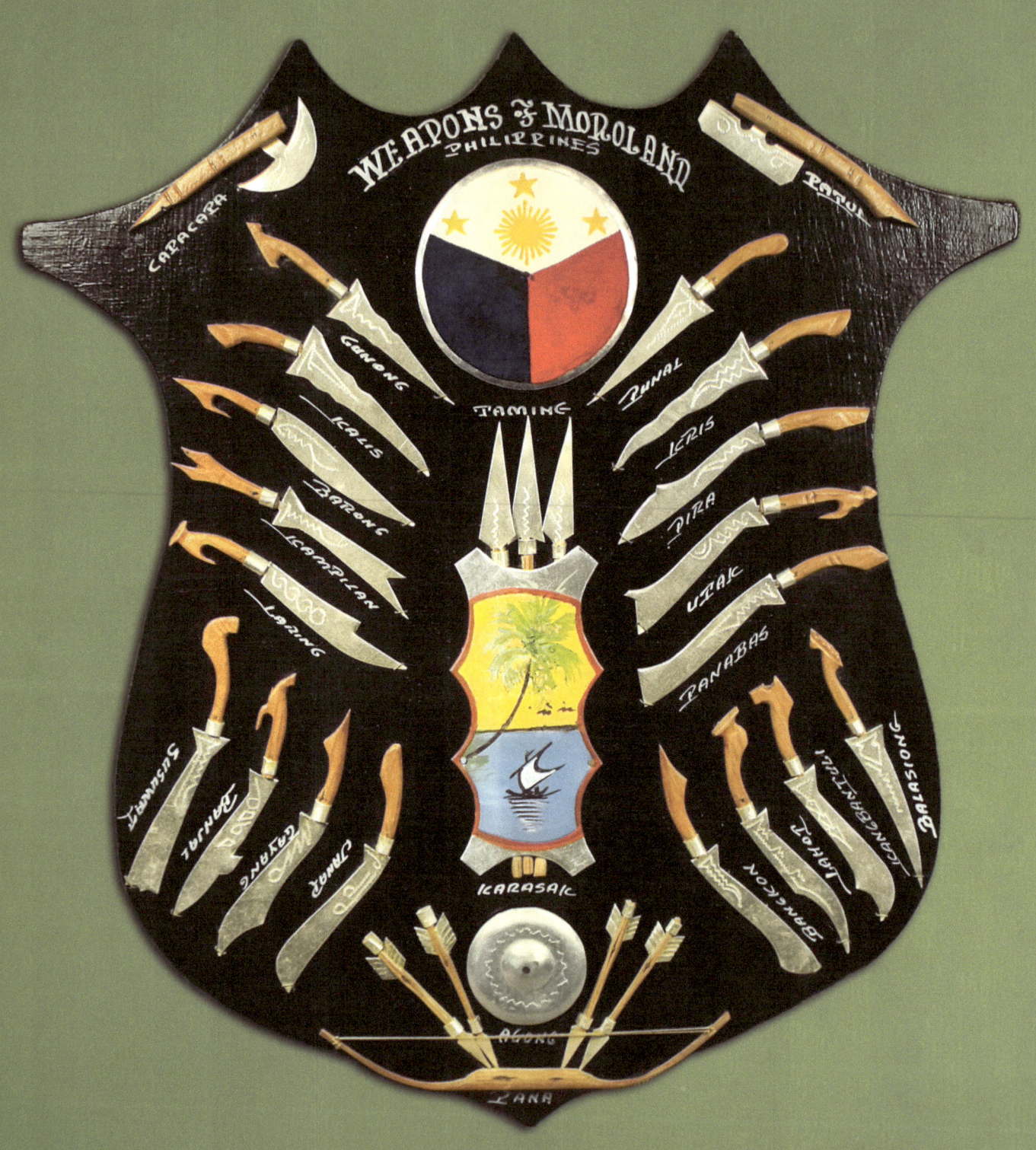

Plaque: #09 Philippines Moro Weapons

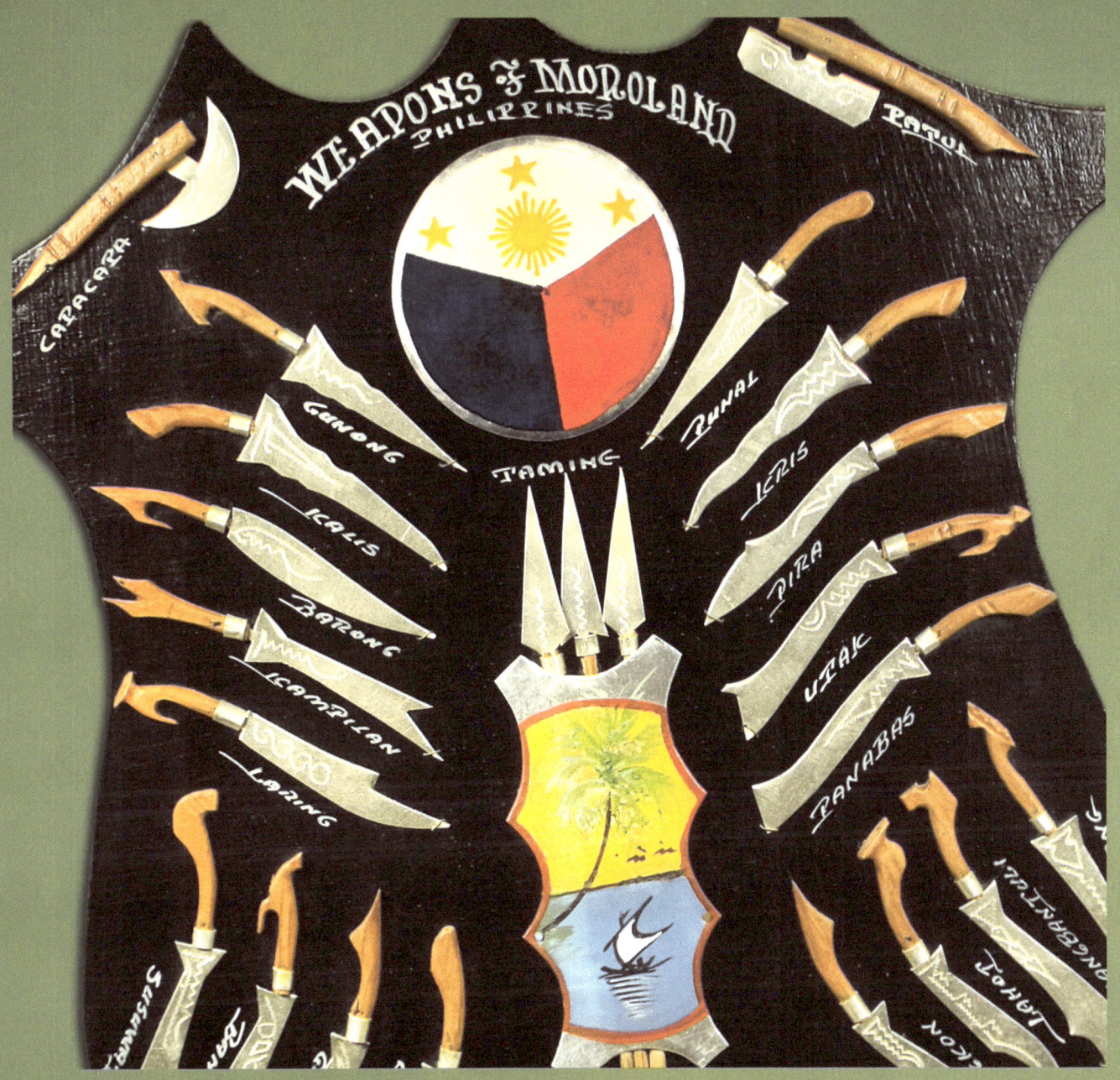

Plaque: #09 Philippines Moro Weapons

Description:

    Miniature Handcrafted Weapons of Moroland Plaque. Handcrafted tourist souvenir made by Filipino natives.

Location Found:	Philippines	**Height:**	14 inches
Location Purchased:	EBay	**Width:**	11.5 inches
Approximate Age:	1970's	**Condition:**	Average

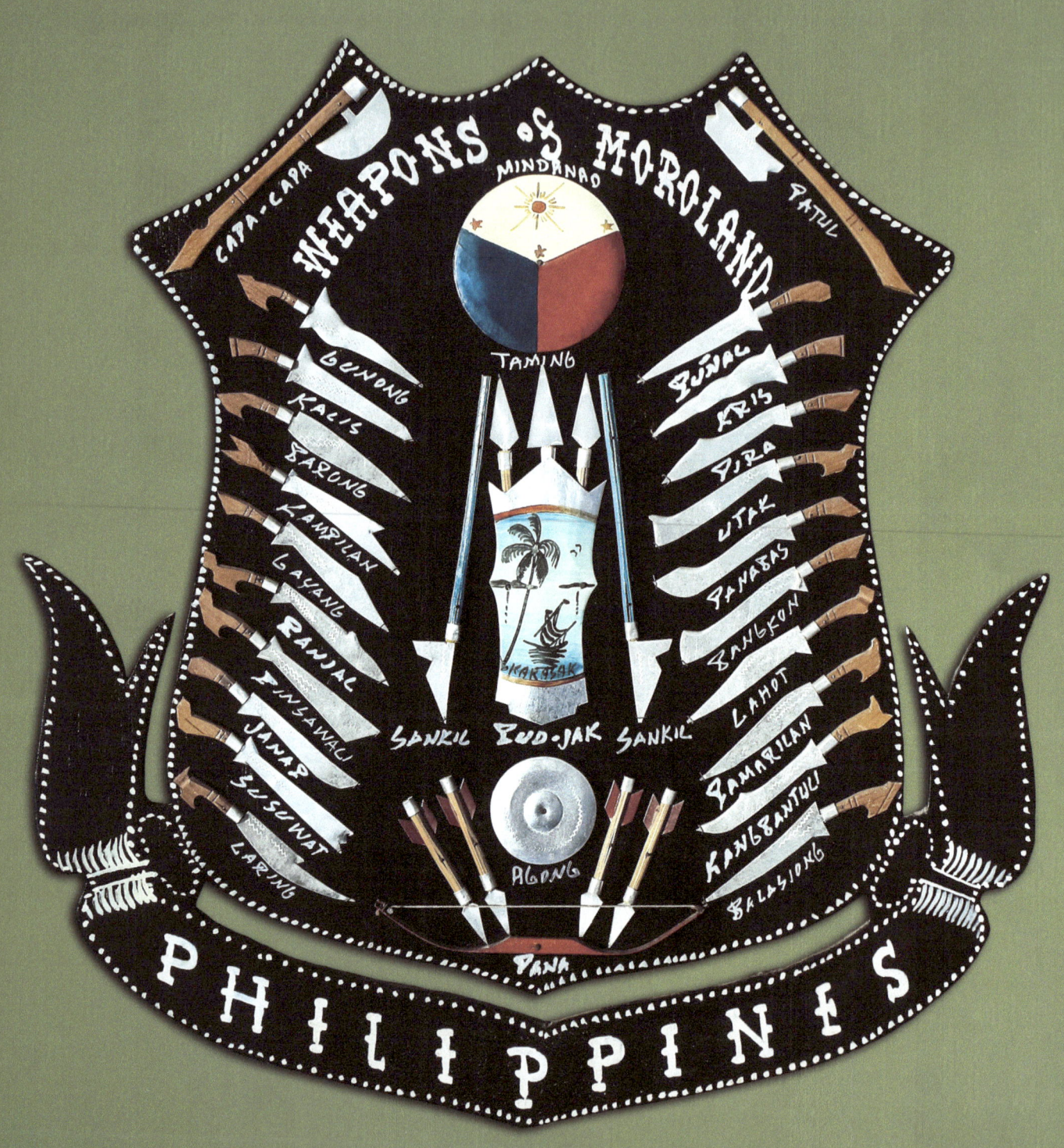

Plaque: #10 Philippines Moro Weapons

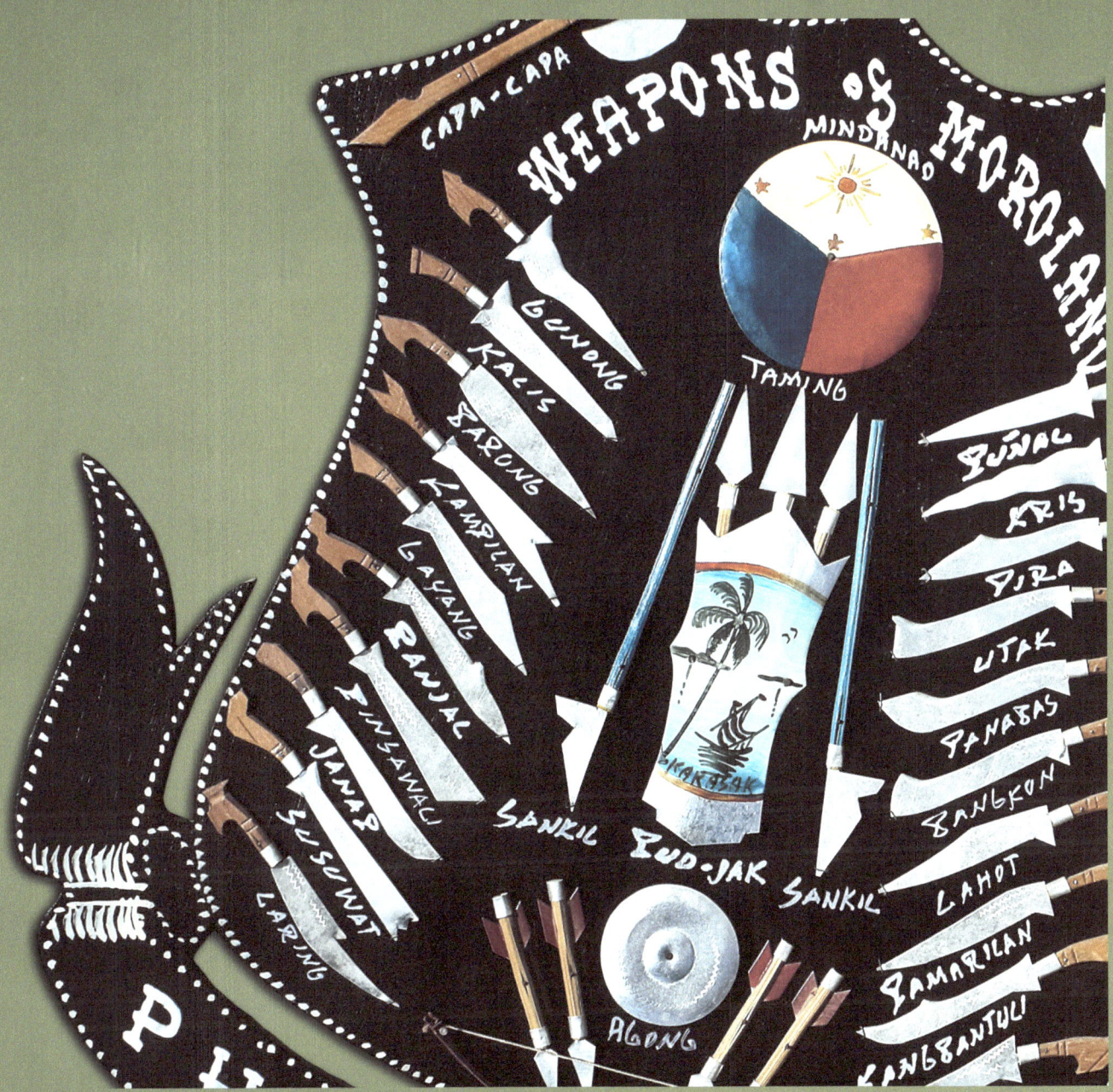

Plaque: #10 Philippines Moro Weapons

Description:
    Weapons of Moroland Display. Handcrafted tourist souvenir made by Filipino natives.

Location Found:	Philippines	**Height:**	14 inches
Location Purchased:	EBay	**Width:**	14 inches
Approximate Age:	1960's	**Condition:**	Above Average

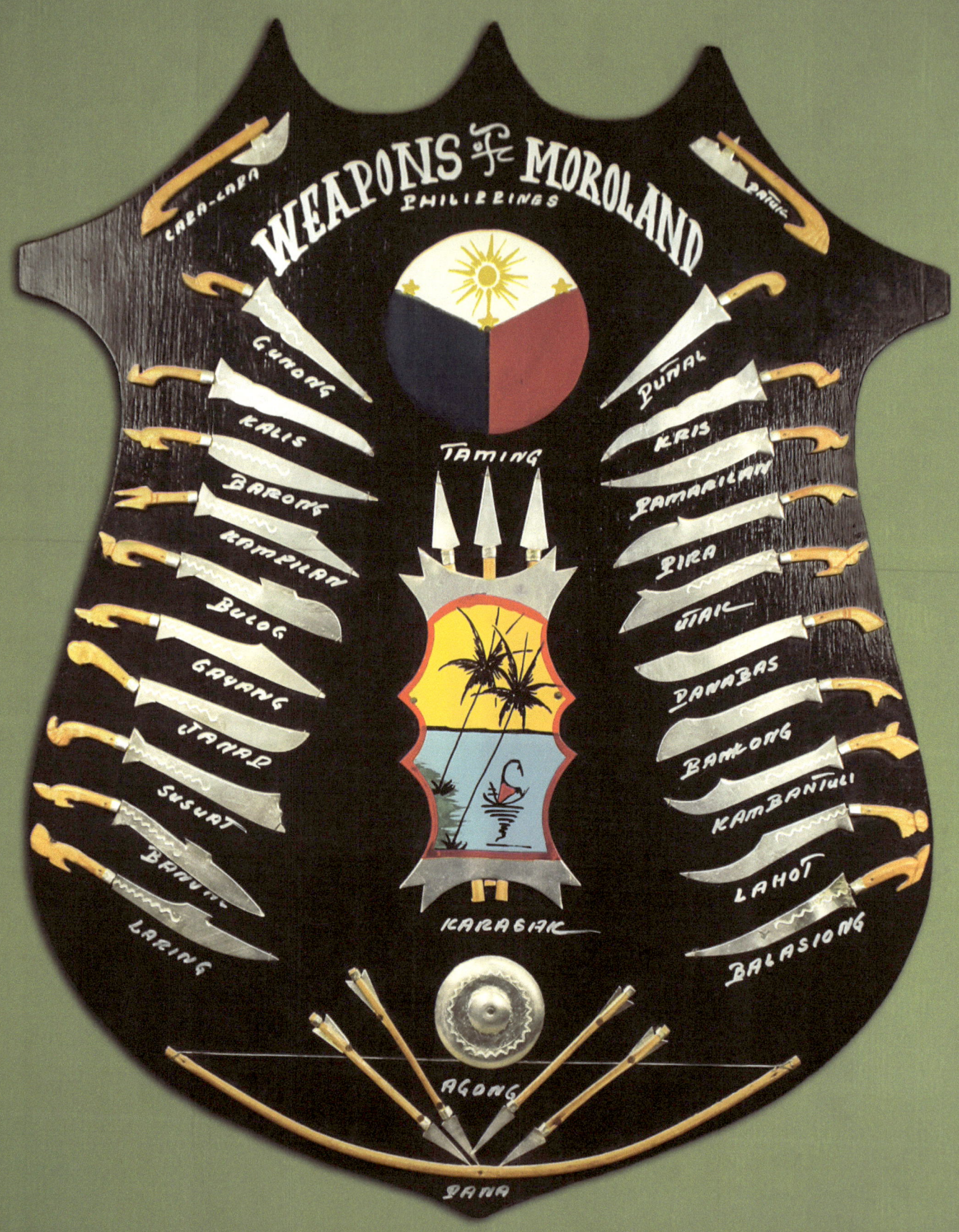

WEAPONS of MOROLAND
PHILIPPINES

Labels on plaque: CARA-CARA, PATUK, GUNONG, PUNAL, KALIS, KRIS, BARONG, LAMARLAW, KAMPILAN, PIRA, BULOG, UTAK, GAYANG, TAMING, DANABAS, JANAP, BAMONG, SUSURT, KAMBANTULI, BANUTE, LAHOT, LARING, KARABAK, BALASIONG, AGONG, BANA

28

Plaque: #11 Philippines Moro Weapons

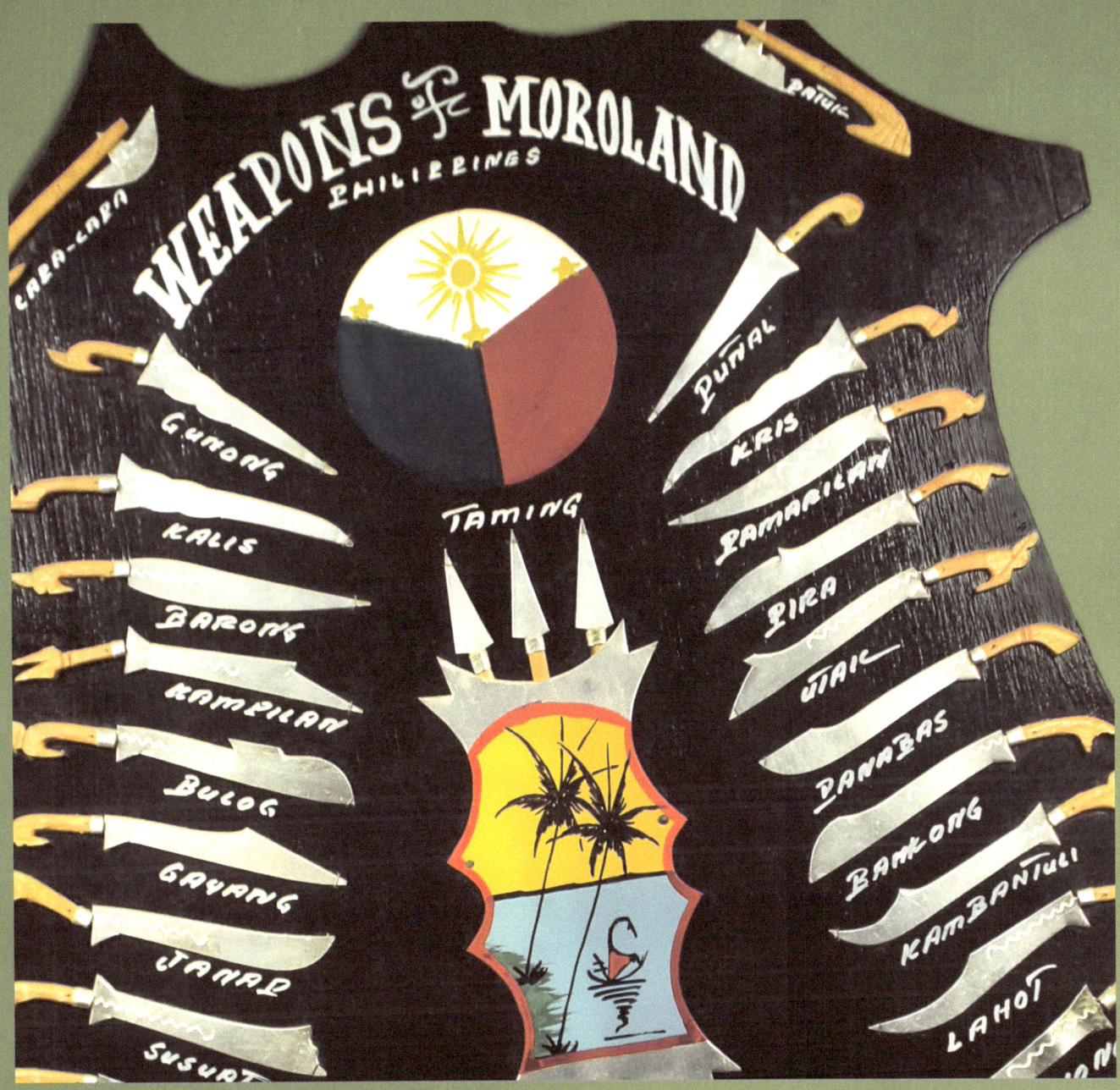

Plaque: #11 Philippines Moro Weapons

Description:
   Weapons of Moroland Display. Handcrafted tourist souvenir made by Filipino natives.

Location Found:	Manila, Philippines	**Height:**	17 inches
Location Purchased:	EBay	**Width:**	13 inches
Approximate Age:	1960's	**Condition:**	Average

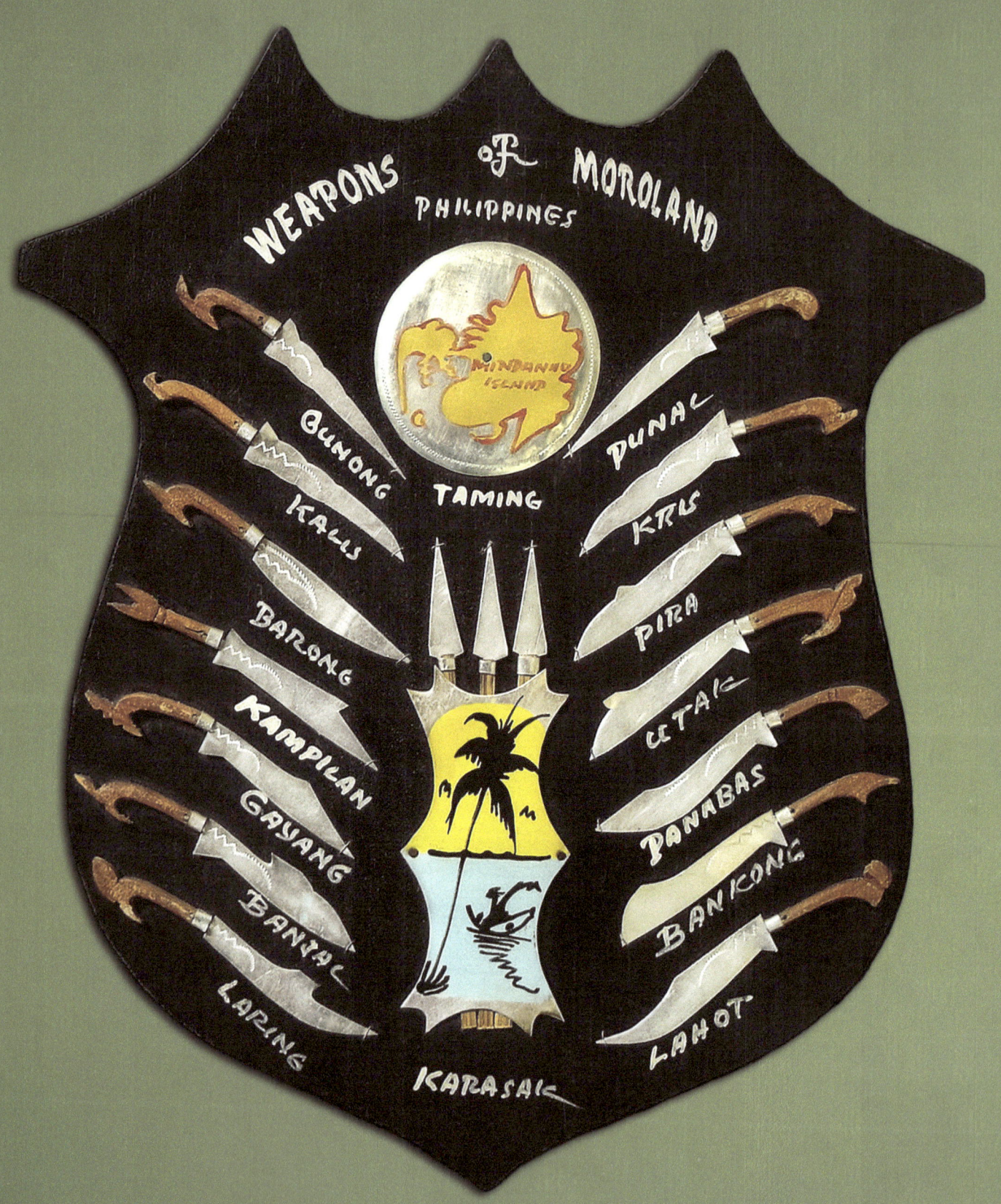

Plaque: #12 Philippines Moro Weapons

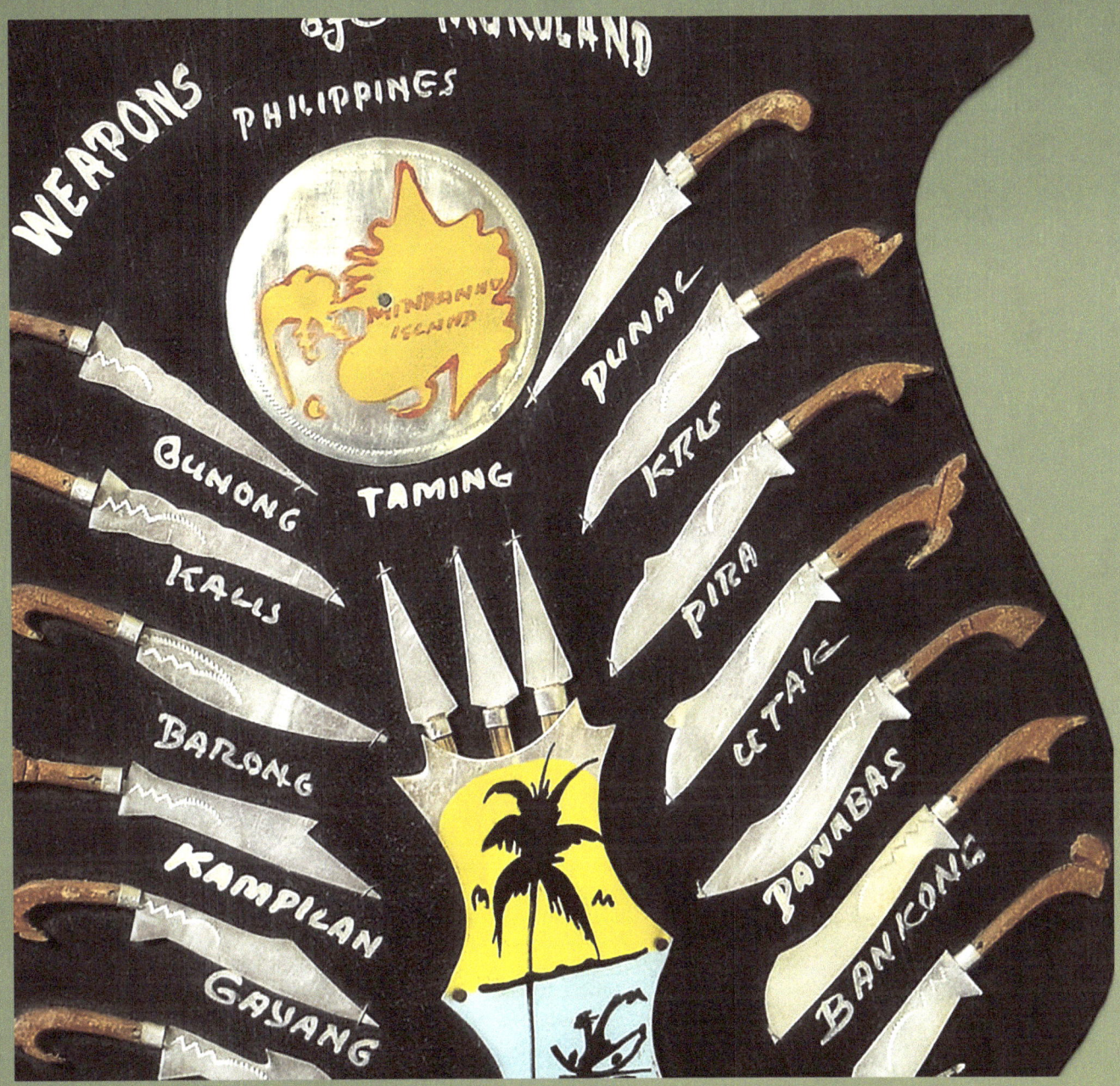

Plaque: #12 Philippines Moro Weapons

Description:

   This is a "Weapons of Moroland" souvenir wall plaque. It is handcrafted from wood by the Filipino natives to be sold to tourists. It has miniature replicas of the ceremonial /combat weapons used by the Moro tribes in the Mindanao region of the Philippines.

Location Found:	Mindanao, Philippines	**Height:**	10.5 inches
Location Purchased:	EBay	**Width:**	8 inches
Approximate Age:	1960's	**Condition:**	Museum Quality

31

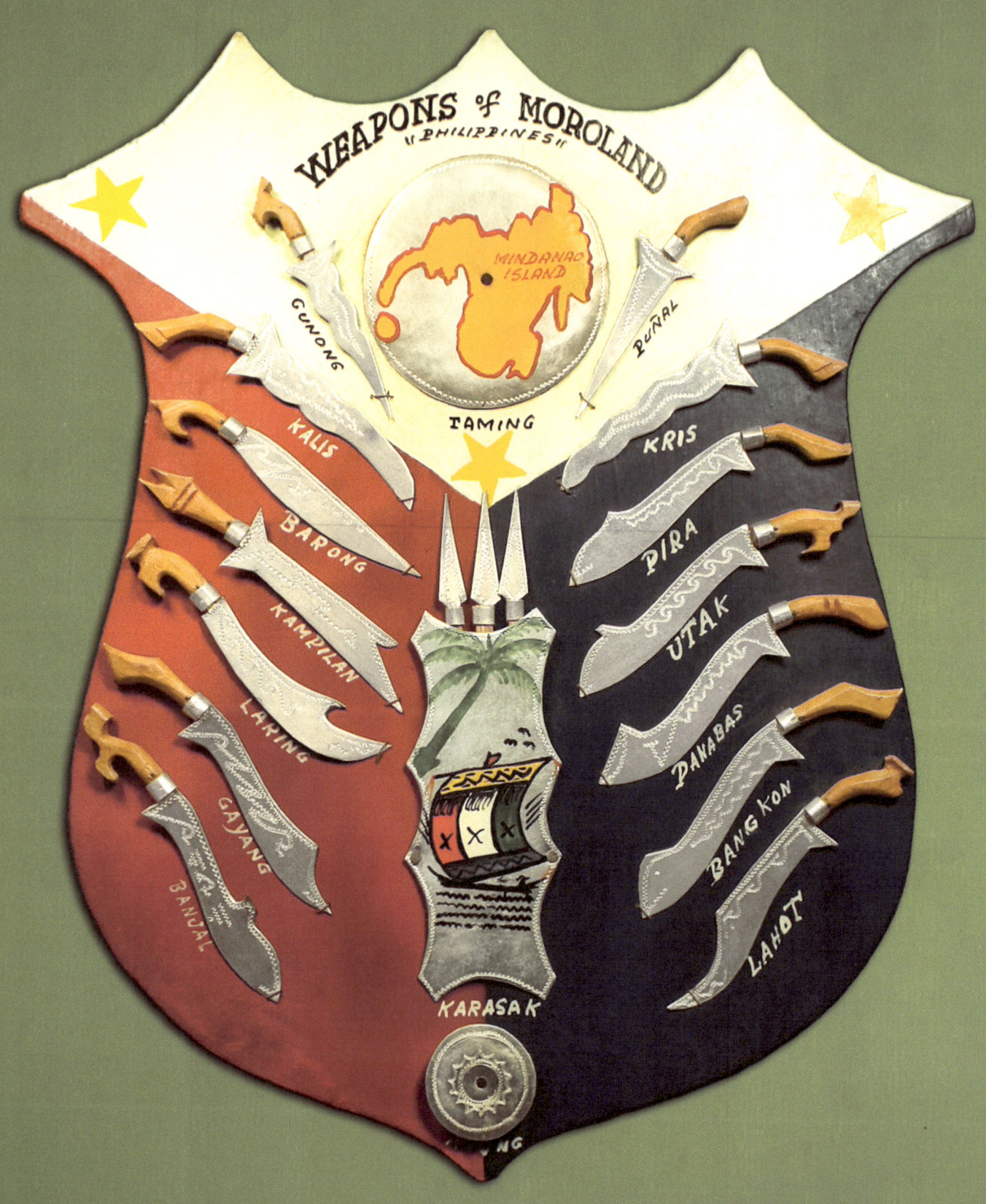

Plaque: #13 Philippines Moro Weapons

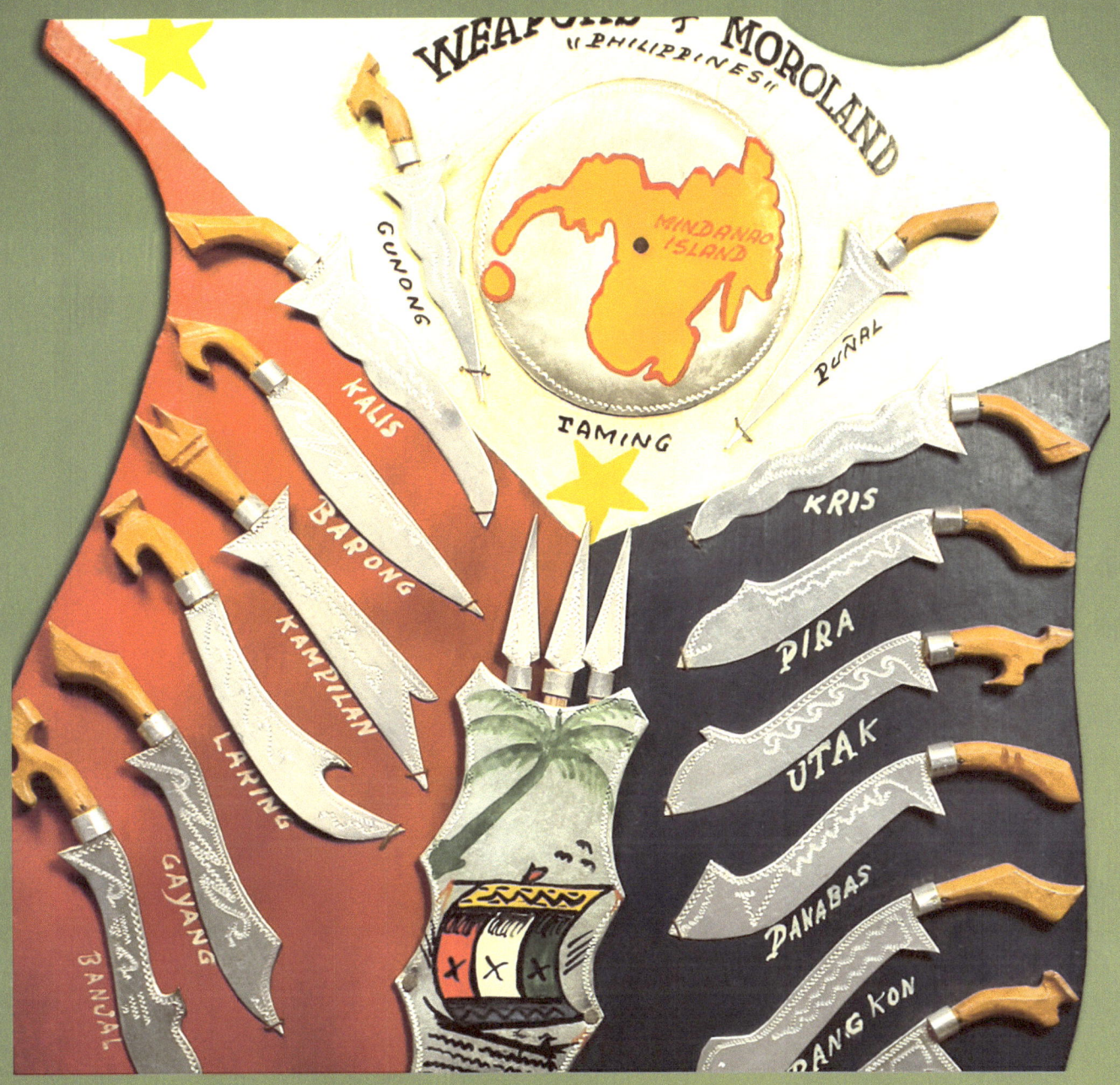

Plaque: #13 Philippines Moro Weapons

Description:

   Handcrafted weapons of the Moro tribe wooden plaque showing 17 miniature hand made weapons from Philippines. This is a hand painted wall plaque and is in great condition with slight edge wear. The top round plate has a painted picture of the island. The middle piece has a beautiful hand painted ship.

Location Found:	Manila, Philippines	**Height:**	11 inches
Location Purchased:	EBay	**Width:**	9 inches
Approximate Age:	1960's	**Condition:**	Above Average

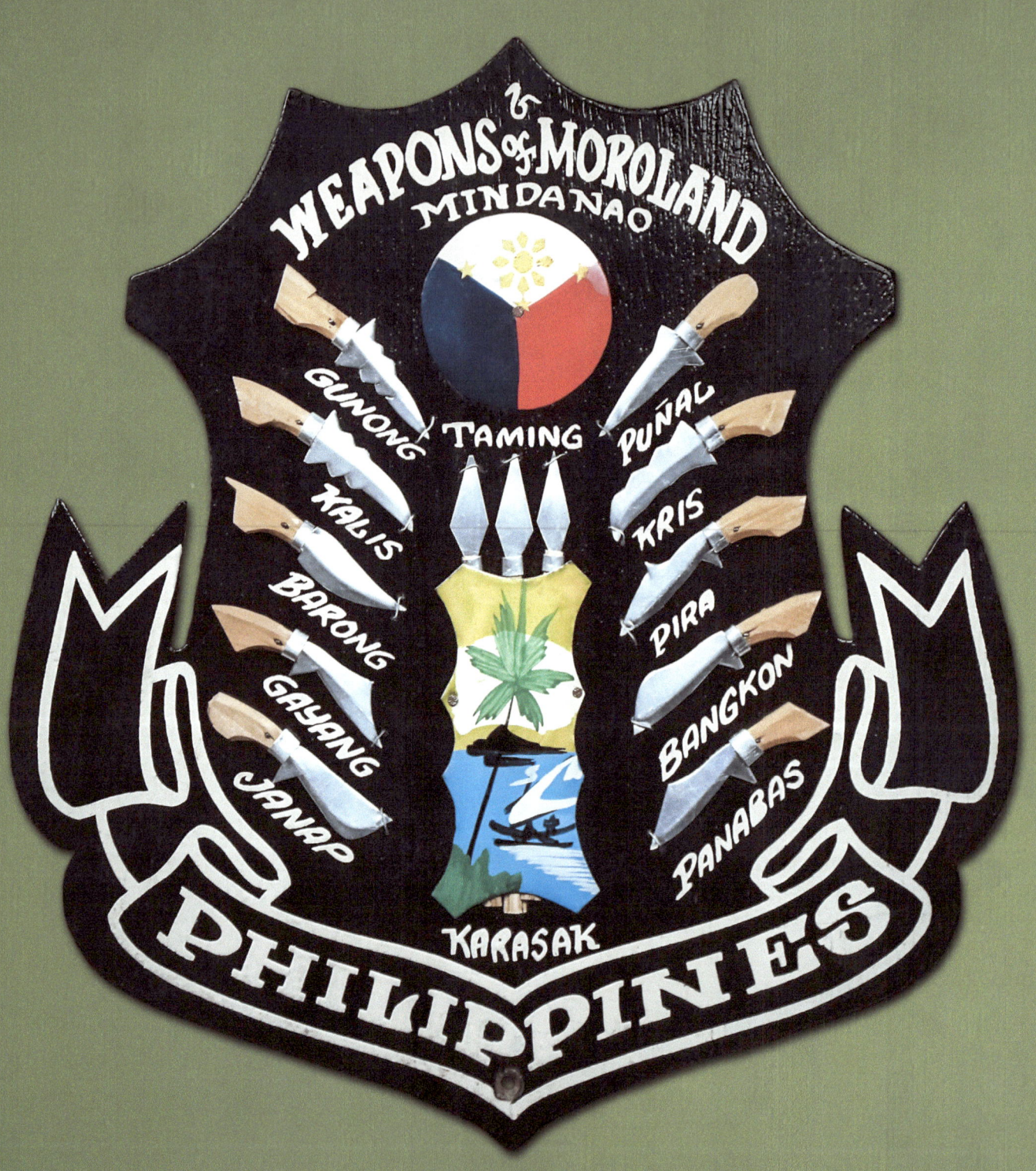

Plaque: #14 Philippines Moro Weapons

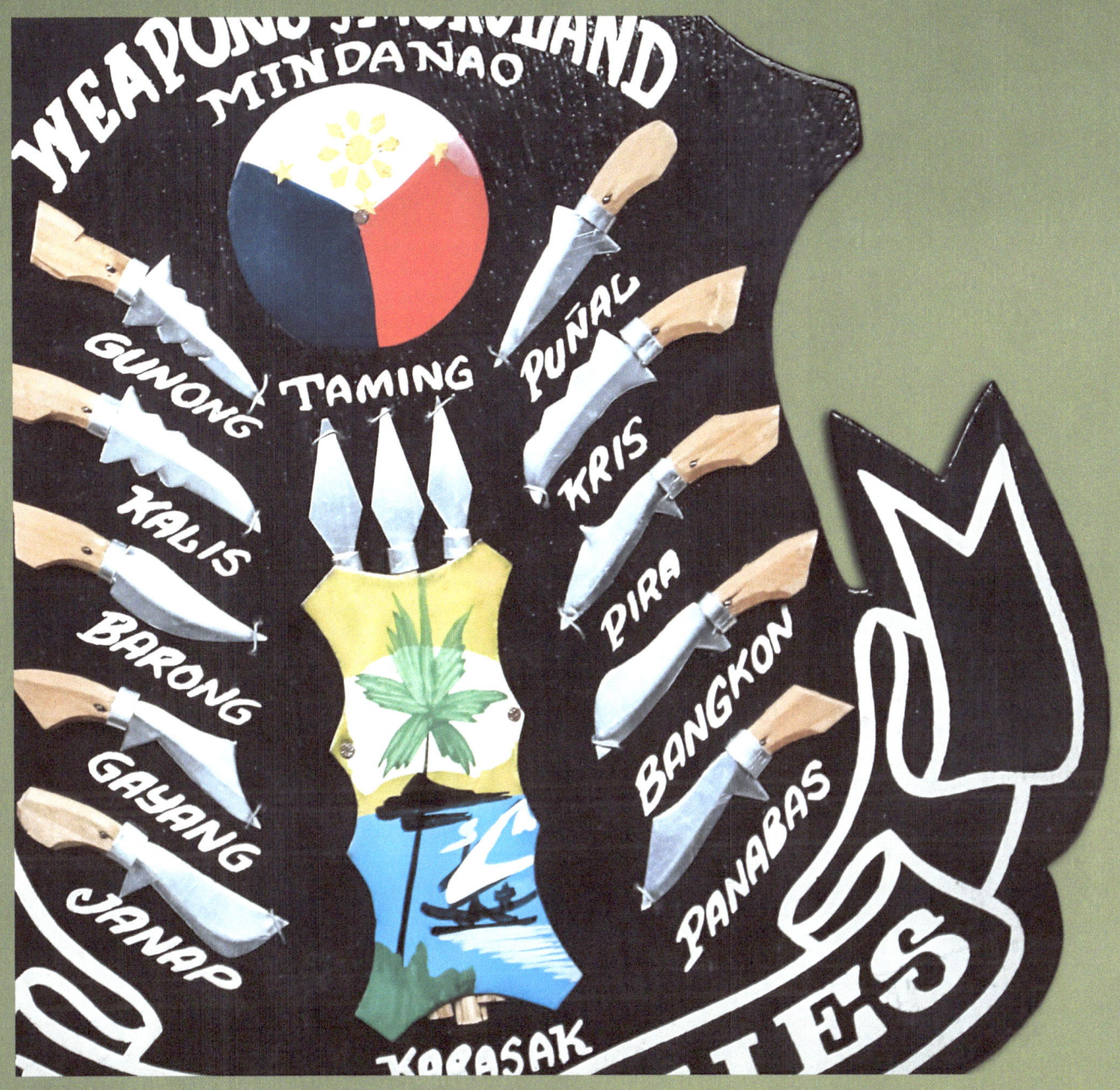

Plaque: #14 Philippines Moro Weapons

Description :

    Small wooden, handcrafted, miniature "Weapons of Moroland" plaque showing many types of Moro tribe blades and weapons. This handcrafted and hand painted plaque is made in the Philippines. The weapons are made of thin aluminum and carved wooden handles.

Location Found:	Manila, Philippines	**Height:**	8.25 inches
Location Purchased:	EBay	**Width:**	8.5 inches
Approximate Age:	1970's	**Condition:**	Museum Quality

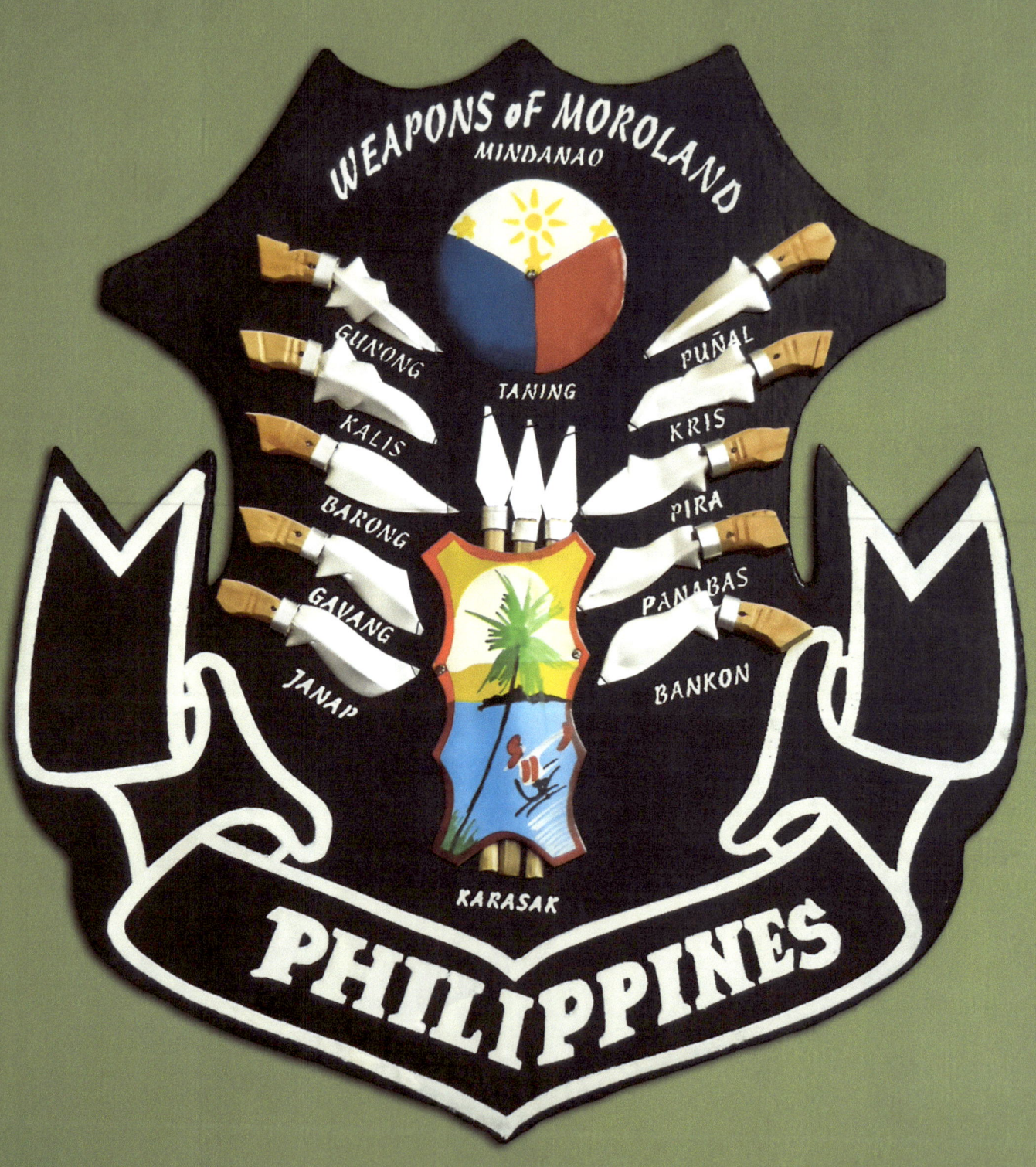

Plaque: #15 Philippines Moro Weapons

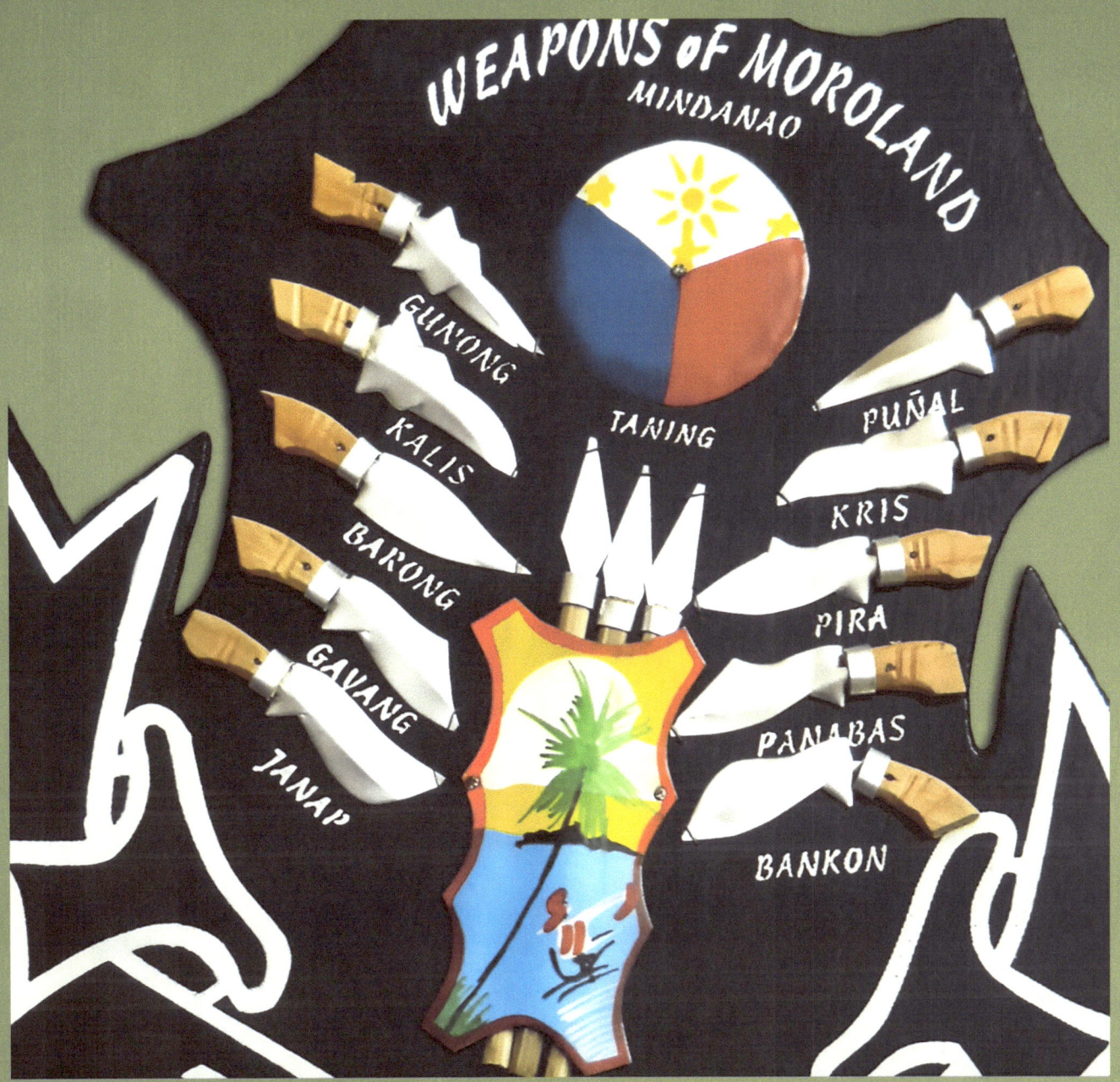

Plaque: #15 Philippines Moro Weapons

Description :

Small wooden, handcrafted, miniature "Weapons of Moroland" plaque showing many types of Moro tribe blades and weapons. This handcrafted and hand painted plaque is made in the Philippines. The weapons are made of thin aluminum and carved wooden handles.

Location Found:	Manila, Philippines	**Height:**	6 inches
Location Purchased:	EBay	**Width:**	8 inches
Approximate Age:	1990's	**Condition:**	Museum Quality

37

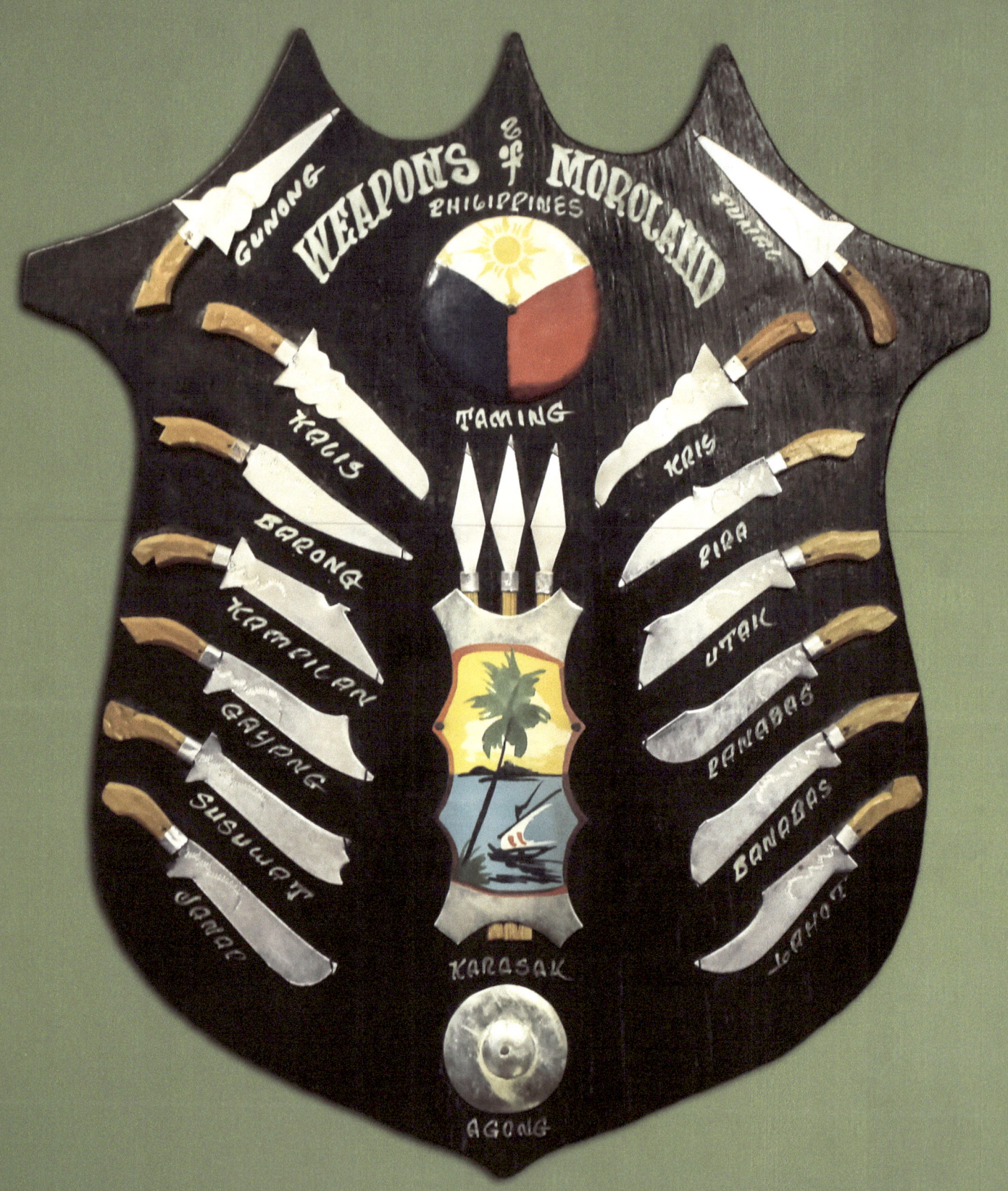

Plaque: #16 Philippines Moro Weapons

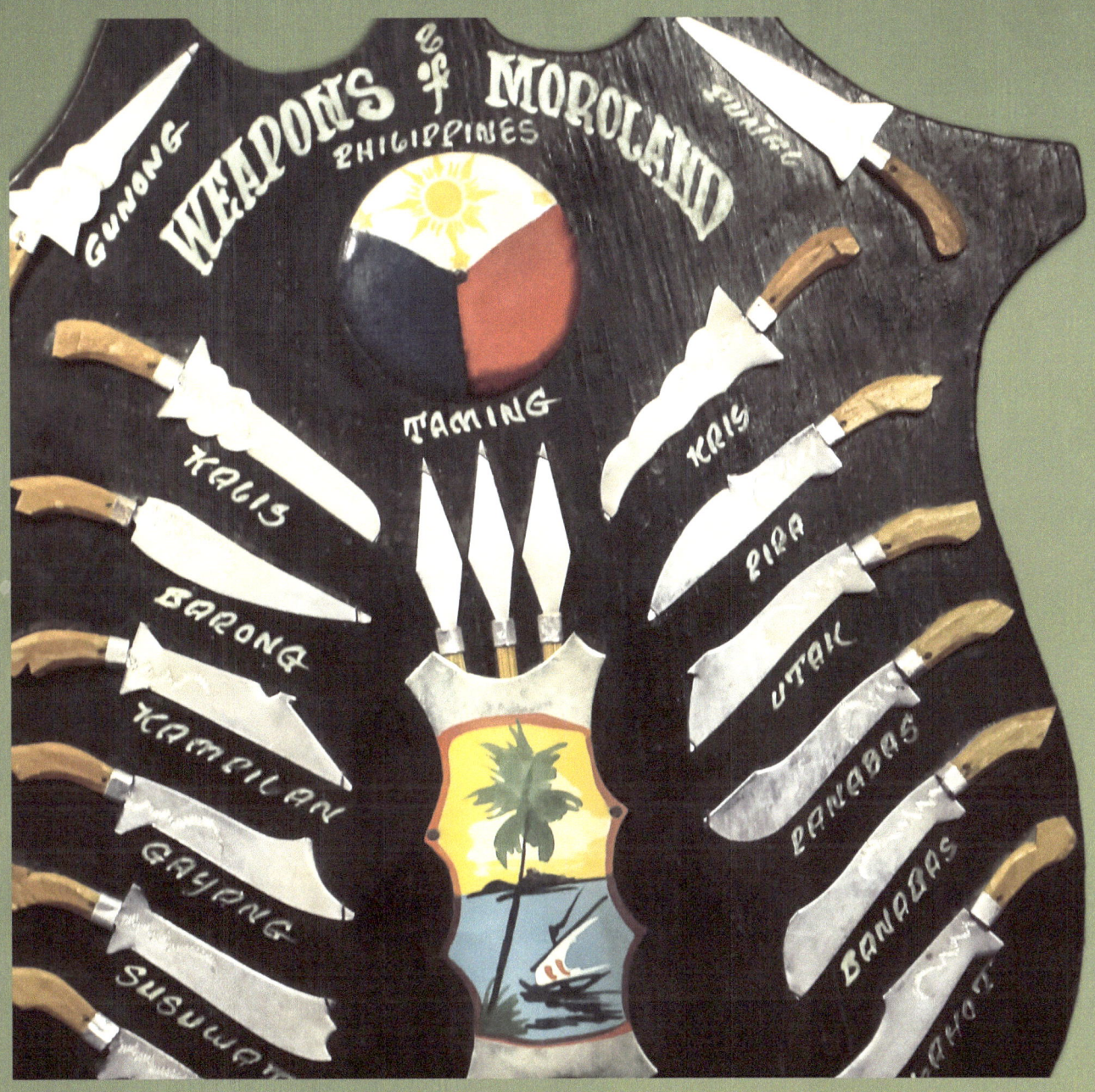

Plaque: #16 Philippines Moro Weapons

Description :
    Handcrafted weapons of the Moro tribe wooden plaque showing many types of weapons from their country.

Location Found:	Cebu, Philippines	**Height:**	10.25 inches
Location Purchased:	EBay	**Width:**	9 inches
Approximate Age:	1970's	**Condition:**	Average

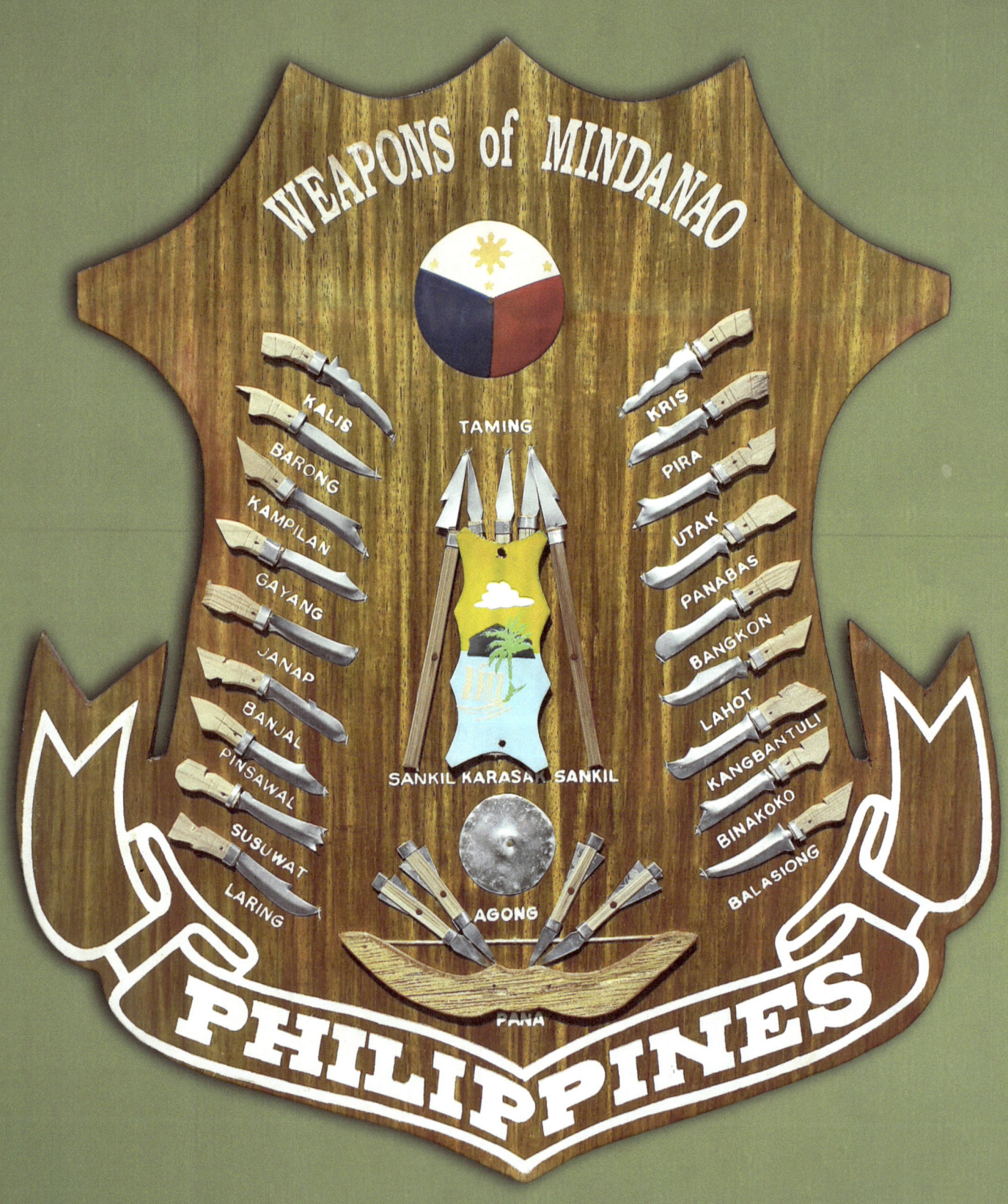

Plaque: #17 Philippines Moro Weapons

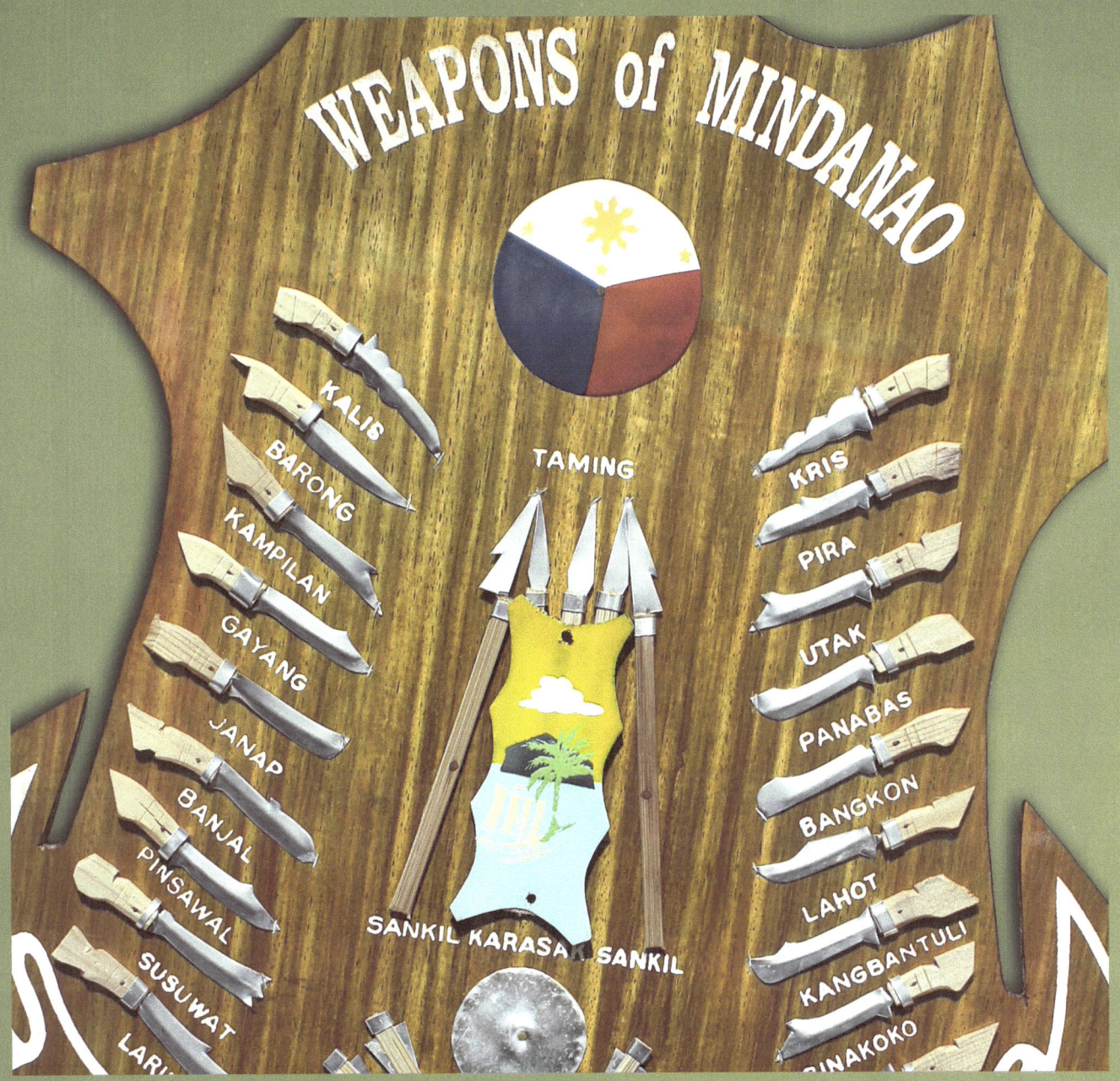

Plaque: #17 Philippines Moro Weapons

Description:

    This is a "Weapons of Mindanao" souvenir wall plaque. It is handcrafted from wood by the Filipino natives to be sold to tourists. It has miniature replicas of the ceremonial/combat weapons used by the Moro tribes in the Mindanao region of the Philippines.

Location Found:	Mindanao, Philippines	**Height:**	17.5 inches
Location Purchased:	EBay	**Width:**	14 inches
Approximate Age:	1990 - 2000	**Condition:**	Above Average

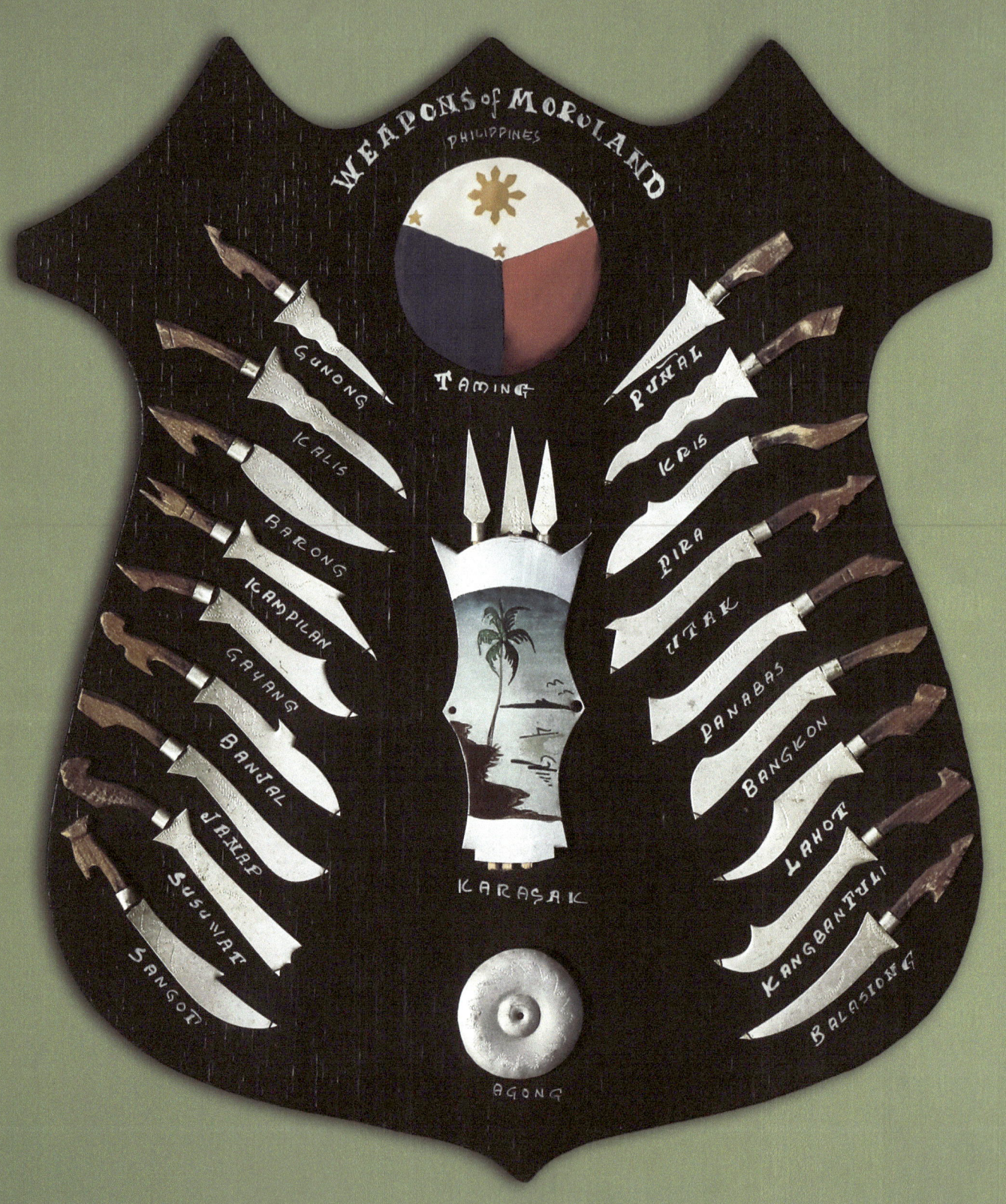

Plaque: #18 Philippines Moro Weapons

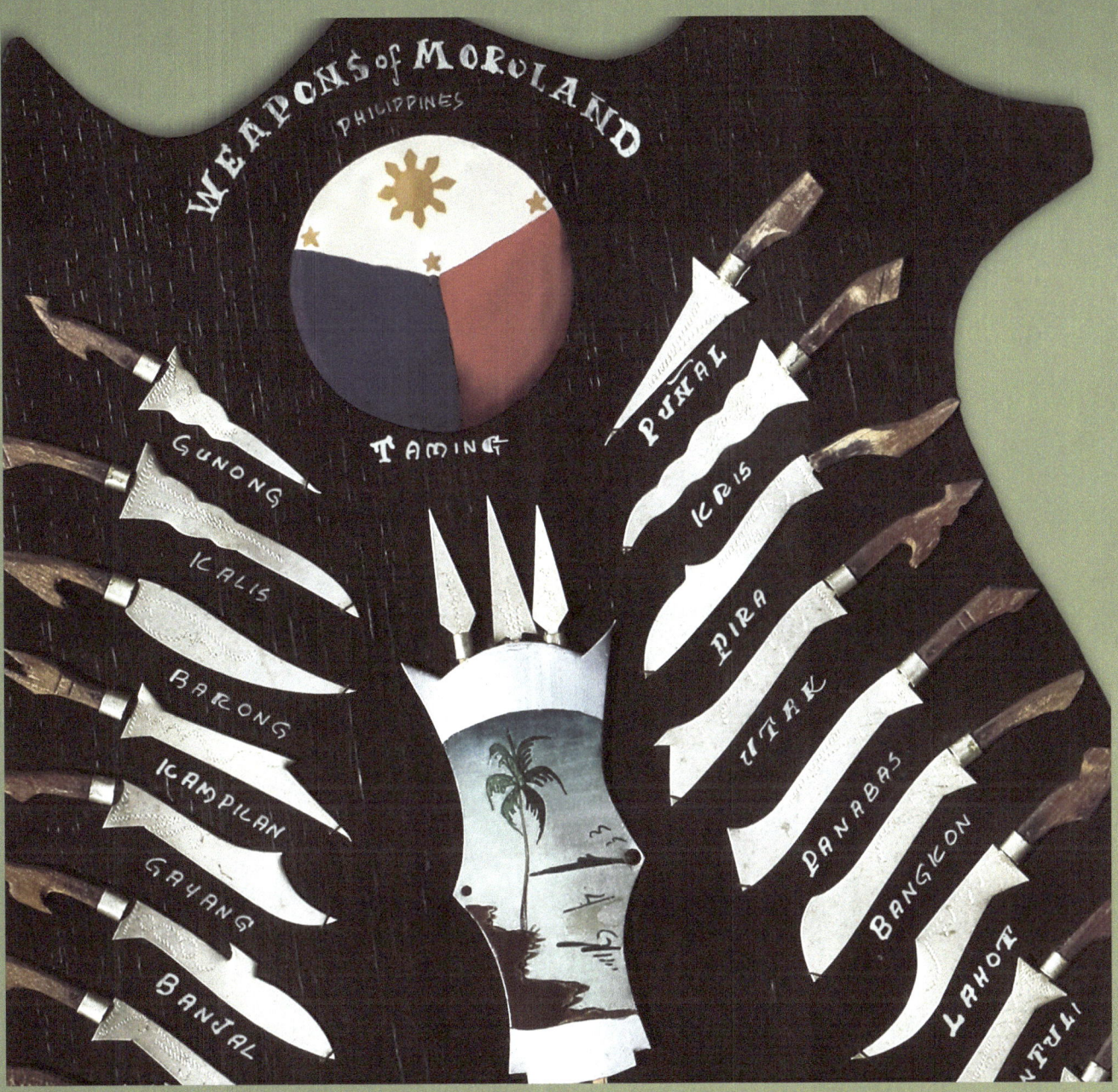

Plaque: #18 Philippines Moro Weapons

Description:
  Old and battered rare hand made hand carved plaque of Philippines weapons.

Location Found:	Philippines	**Height:**	13 inches
Location Purchased:	EBay	**Width:**	11.5 inches
Approximate Age:	1940's	**Condition:**	Average

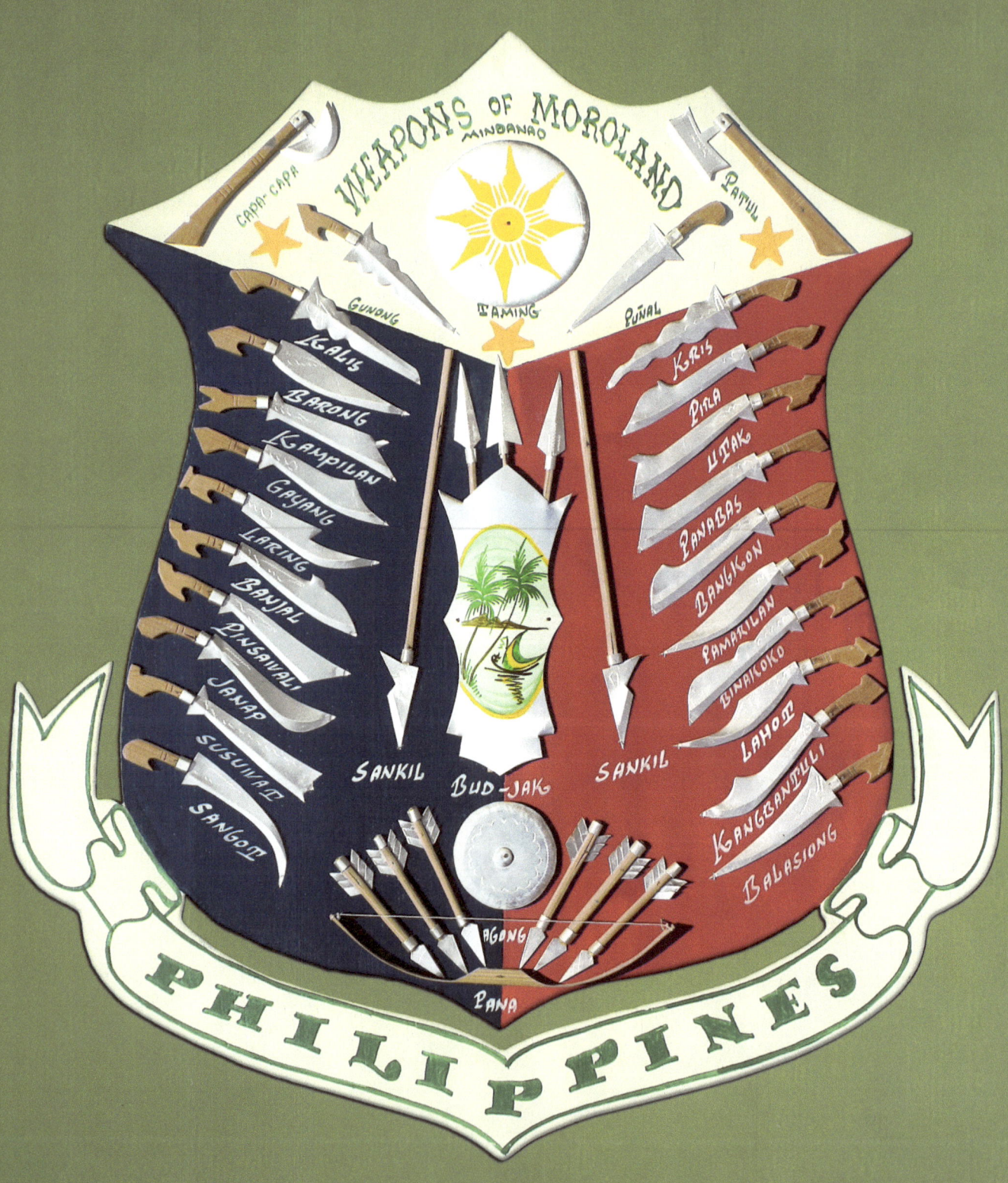

Plaque: #19 Philippines Moro Weapons

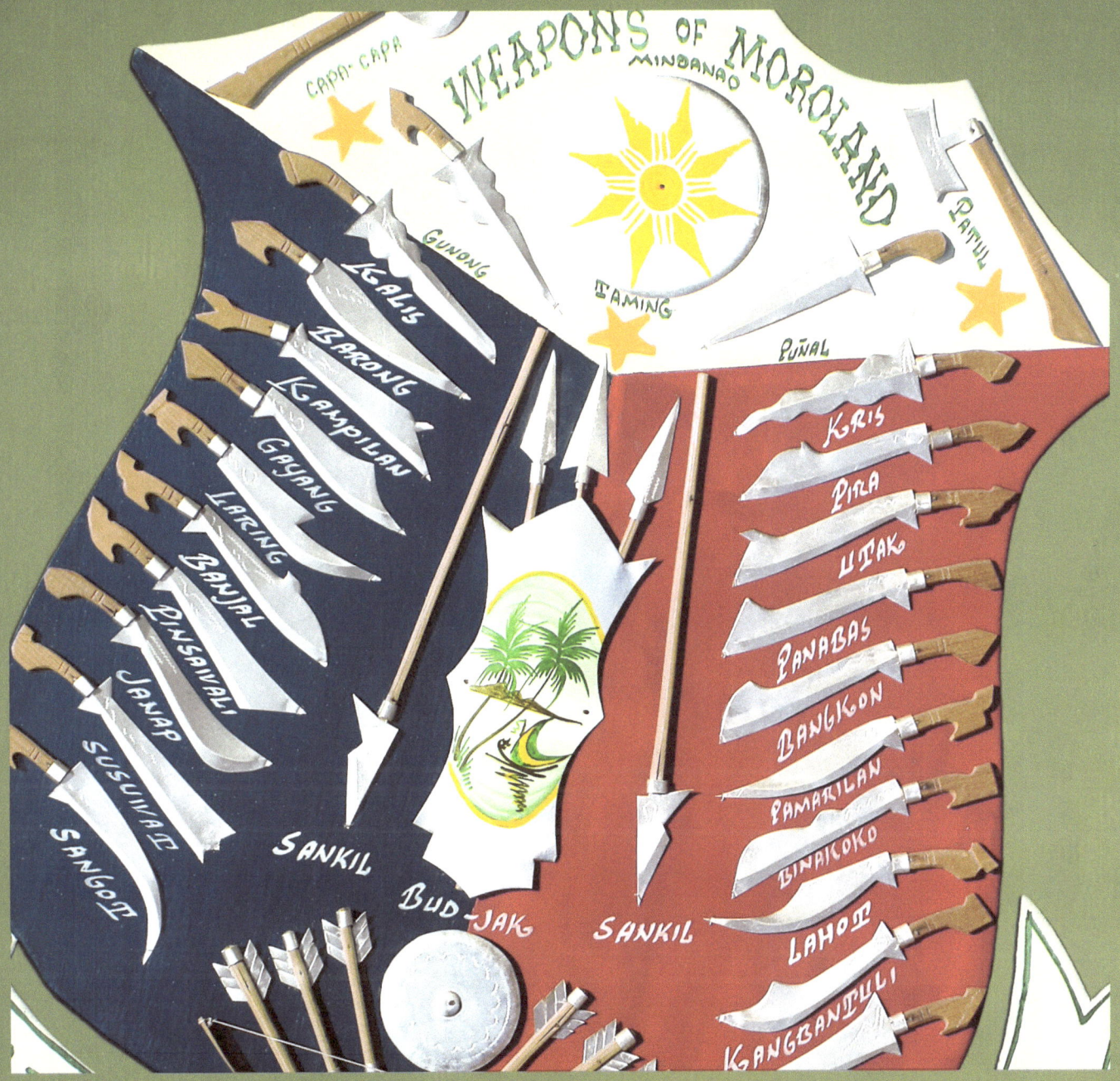

Plaque: #19 Philippines Moro Weapons

Description:

    This is a "Weapons of Moroland" souvenir wall plaque. It is handcrafted from wood by the Filipino natives to be sold to tourists. It has miniature replicas of the ceremonial/combat weapons used by the Moro tribes in the Mindanao region of the Philippines.

Location Found:	Mindanao, Philippines	**Height:**	23.5 inches
Location Purchased:	EBay	**Width:**	21.25 inches
Approximate Age:	1950's-1960's	**Condition:**	Above Average

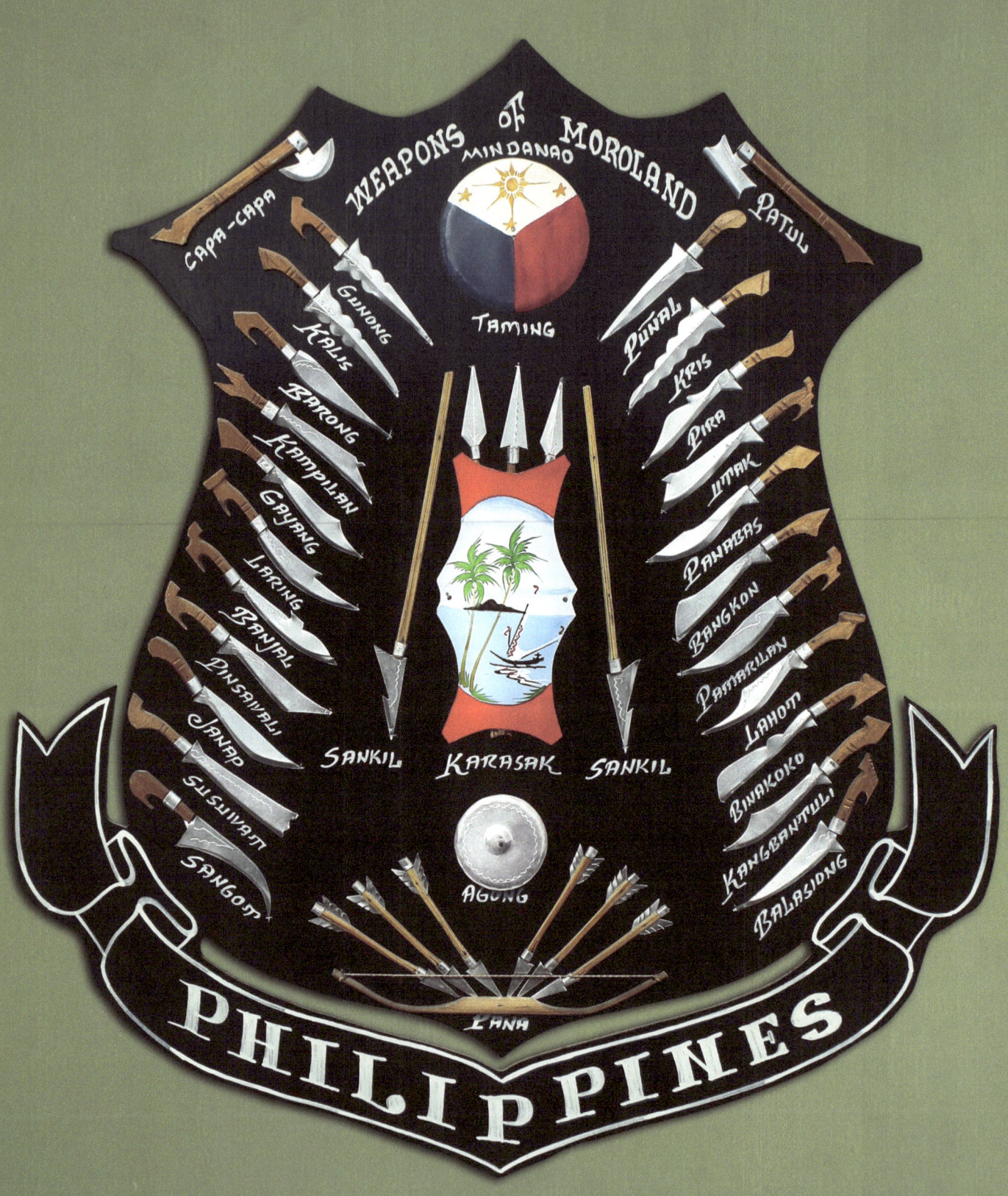

Plaque: #20 Philippines Moro Weapons

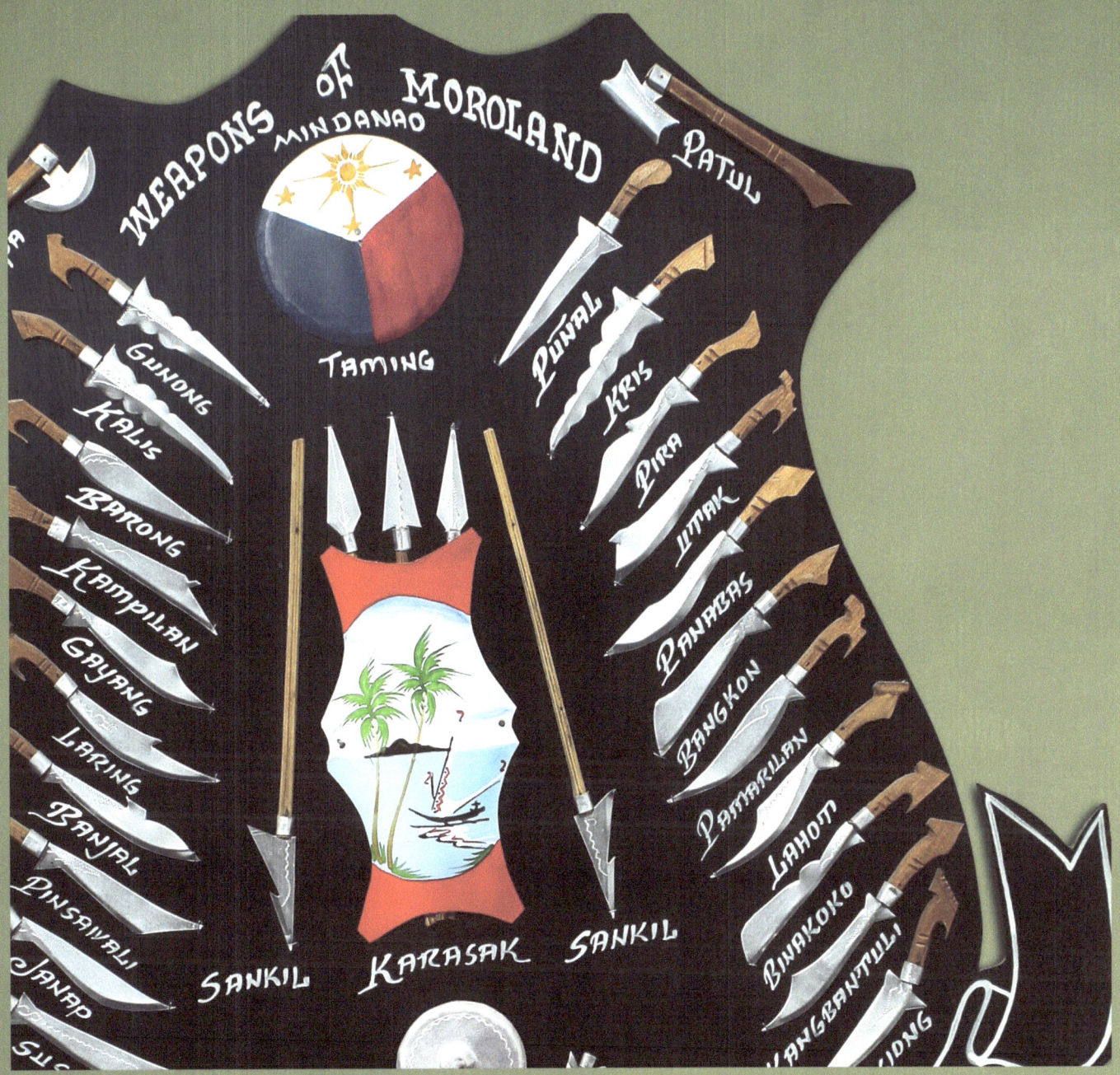

Plaque: #20 Philippines Moro Weapons

Description:

    This is a "Weapons of Moroland" souvenir wall plaque. It is handcrafted from wood by the Filipino natives to be sold to tourists. It has miniature replicas of the ceremonial/combat weapons used by the Moro tribes in the Mindanao region of the Philippines.

Location Found:	Mindanao, Philippines	**Height:**	23.5 inches
Location Purchased:	EBay	**Width:**	21.25 inches
Approximate Age:	1950 – 1960	**Condition:**	Above Average

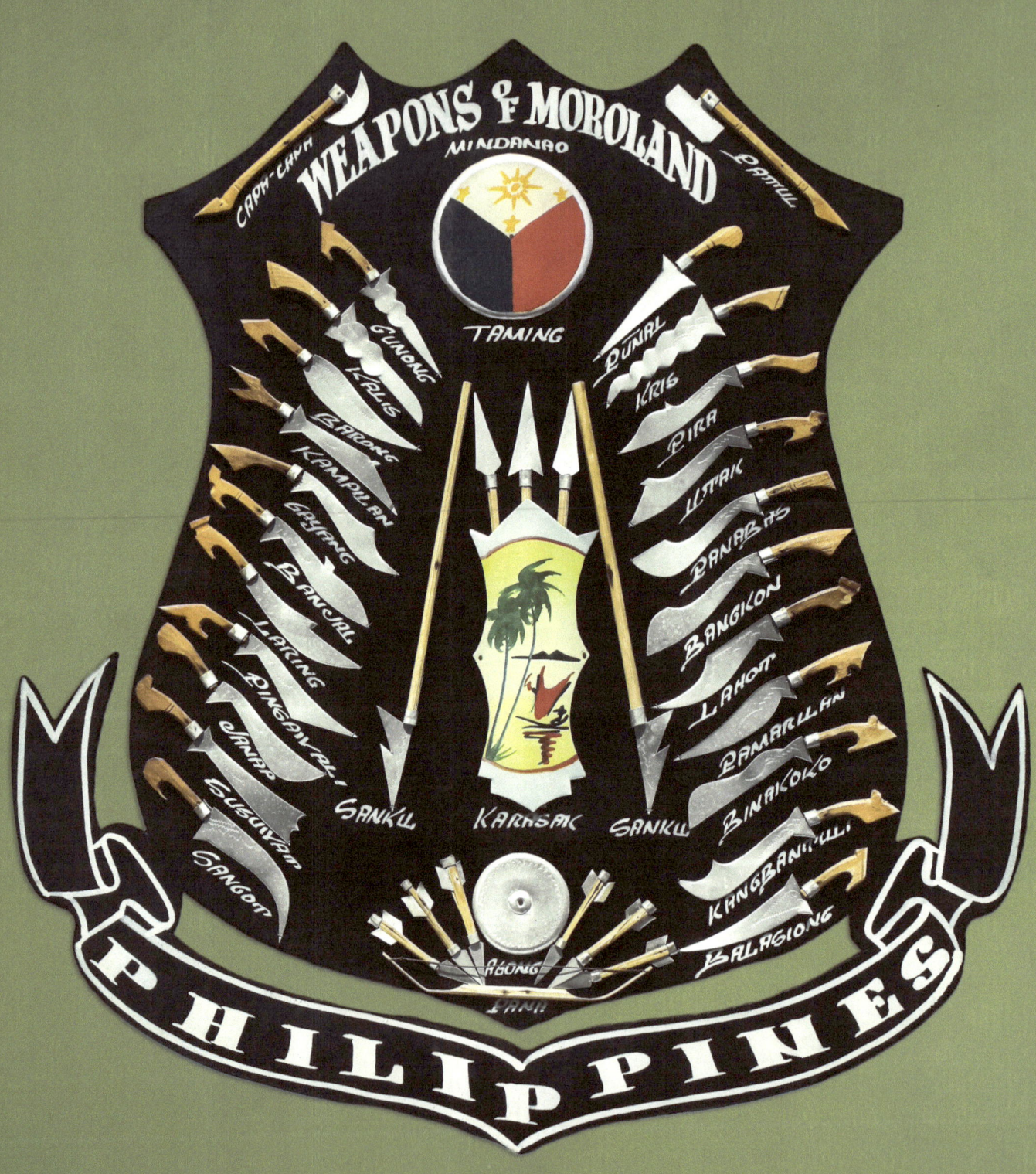

Plaque: #21 Philippines Moro Weapons

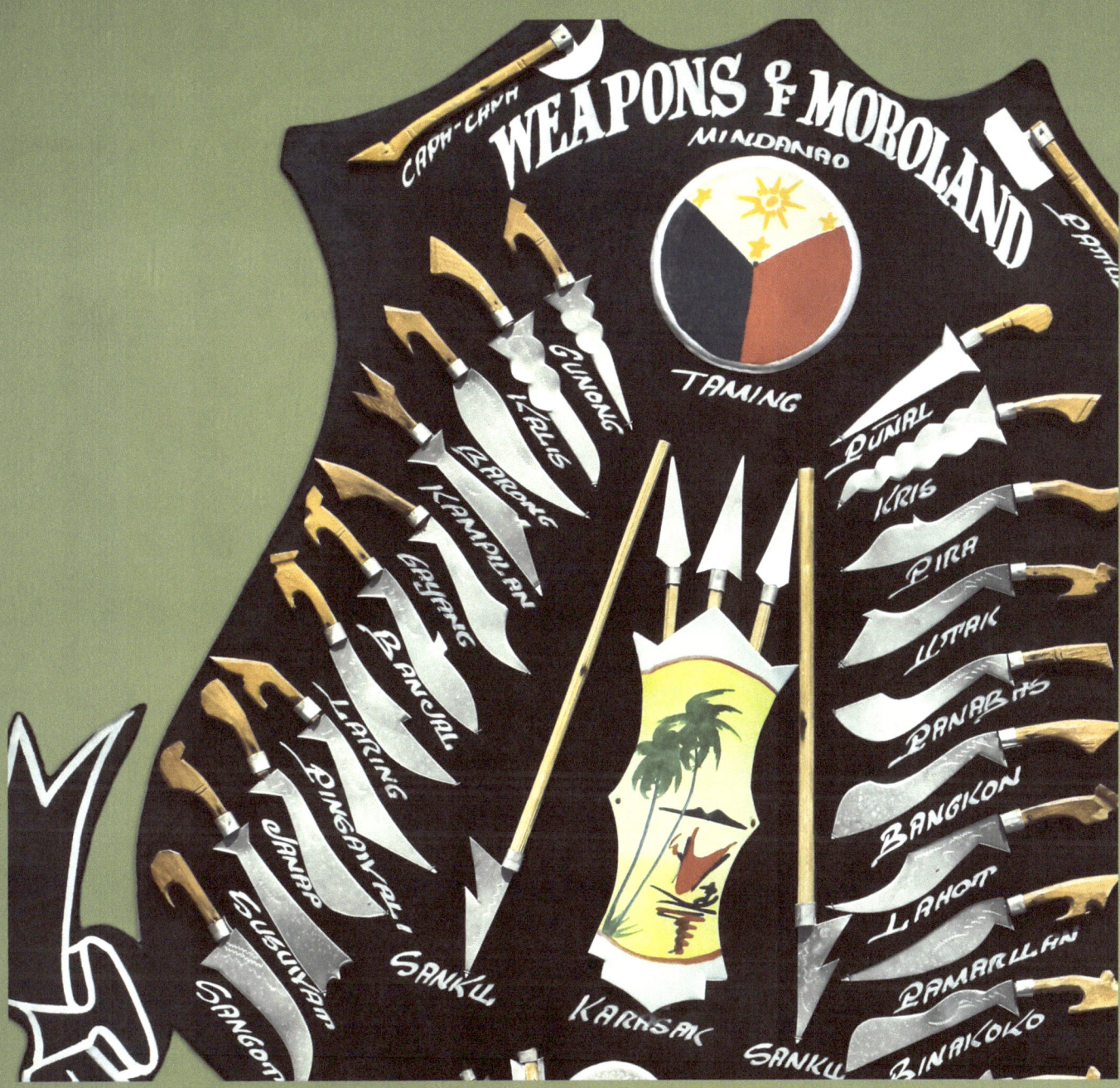

Plaque: #21 Philippines Moro Weapons

Description:

   This is a "Weapons of Moroland" souvenir wall plaque. It is handcrafted from wood by the Filipino natives to be sold to tourists. It has miniature replicas of the ceremonial/combat weapons used by the Moro tribes in the Mindanao region of the Philippines.

Location Found:	Mindanao, Philippines	**Height:**	23.5 inches
Location Purchased:	EBay	**Width:**	21.25 inches
Approximate Age:	1950 – 1960	**Condition:**	Above Average

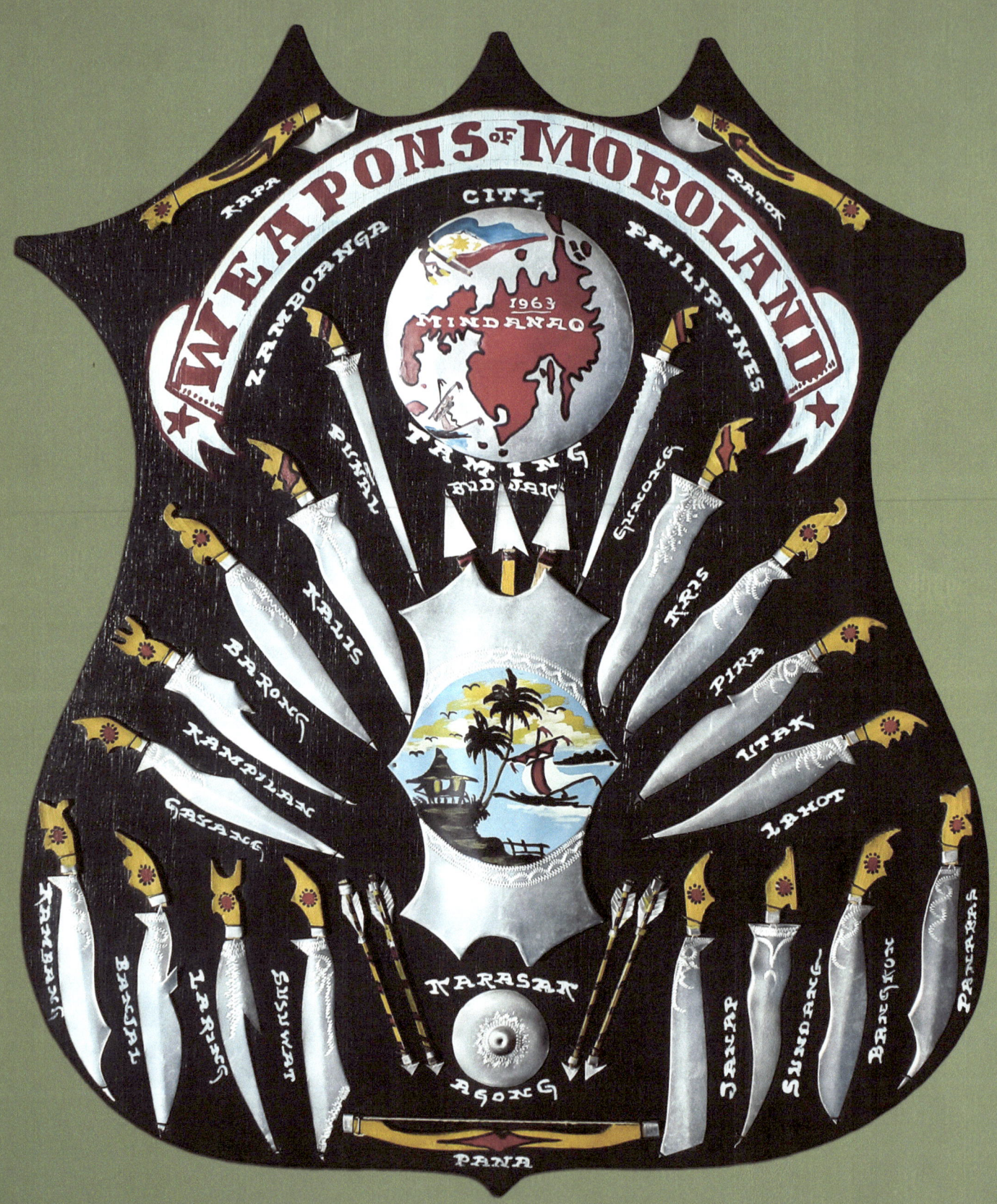

Plaque: #22 Philippines Moro Weapons

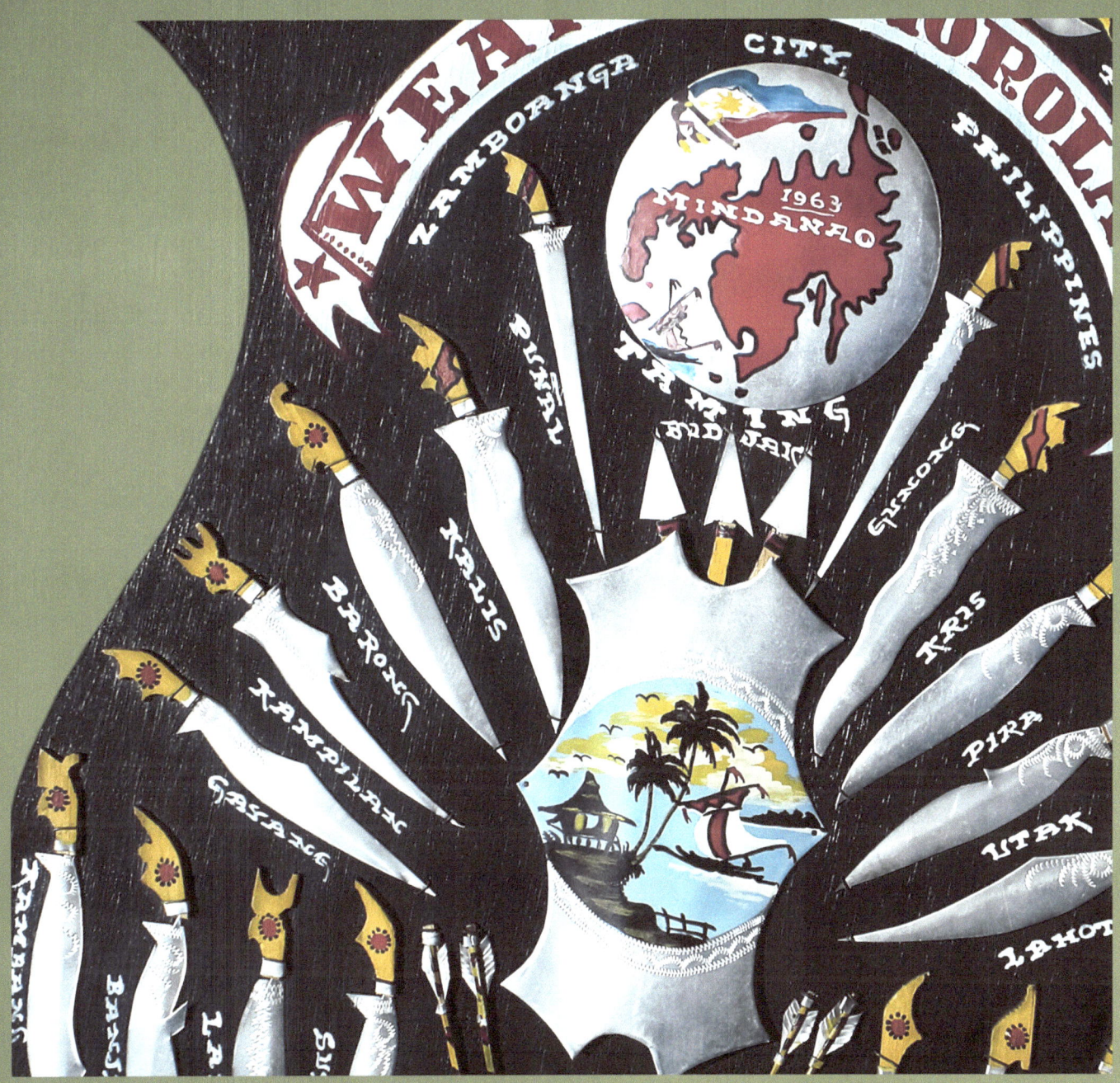

Plaque: #22 Philippines Moro Weapons

Description:

Old and battered rare handmade, handcraved plaque-Weapons Of Moroland Shield. This item was brought back from the Philippines after the Korean war. This wall display features assorted swords, arrows and other weapons. Below the title is: Zamboanga City Philippines and Mindanao 1963.

Location Found:	Zamboanga City, Philippines	**Height:**	22.5 inches
Location Purchased:	EBay	**Width:**	19 inches
Approximate Age:	1963	**Condition:**	Average

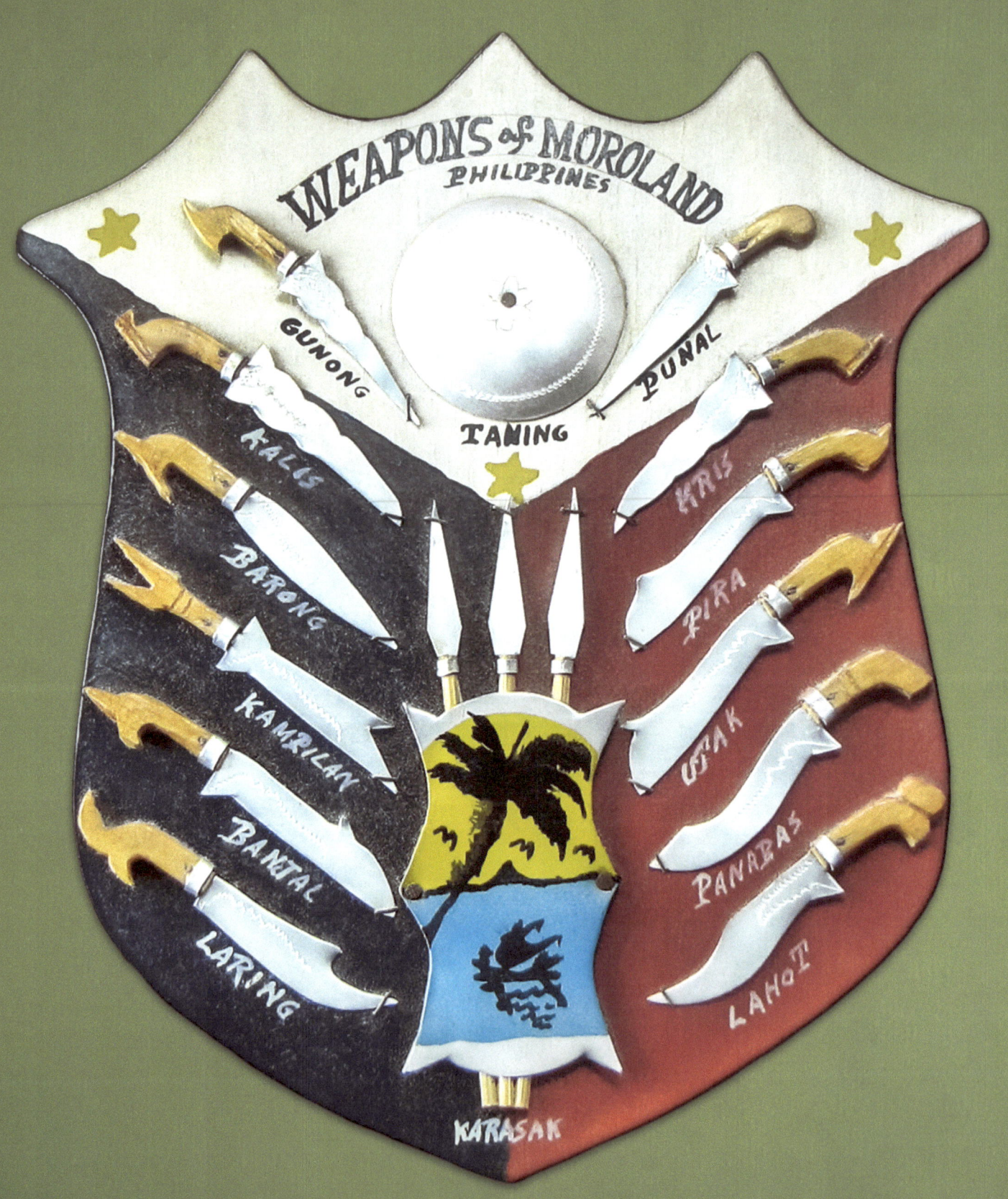

Plaque: #23 Philippines Moro Weapons

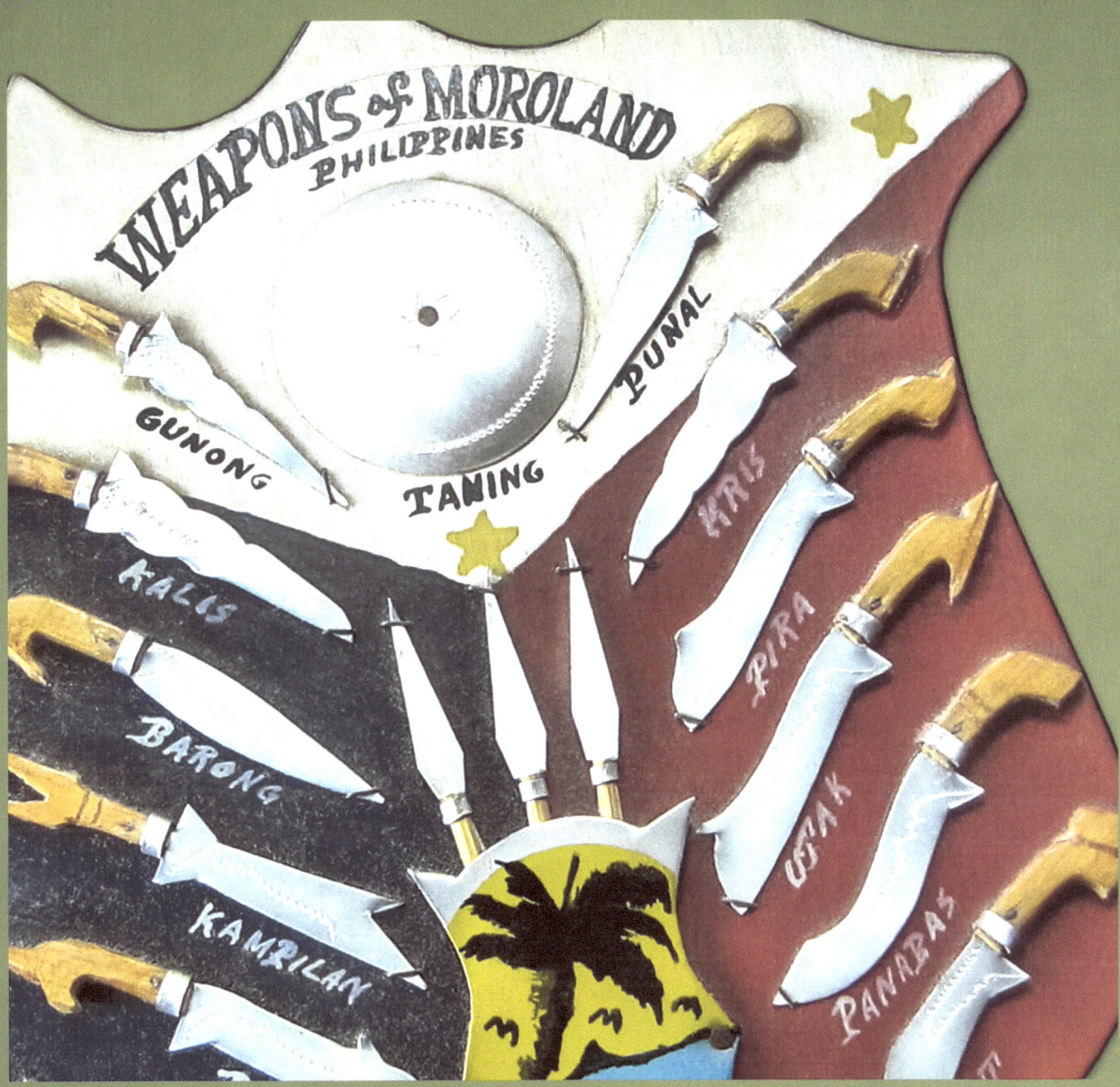

Plaque: #23 Philippines Moro Weapons

Description:

  Vintage handmade Weapons Of Moroland shield. This wall display features assorted swords, arrows and other weapons.

Location Found:	Manila, Philippines	**Height:**	6.75 inches
Location Purchased:	EBay	**Width:**	6 inches
Approximate Age:	1960's	**Condition:**	Above Average

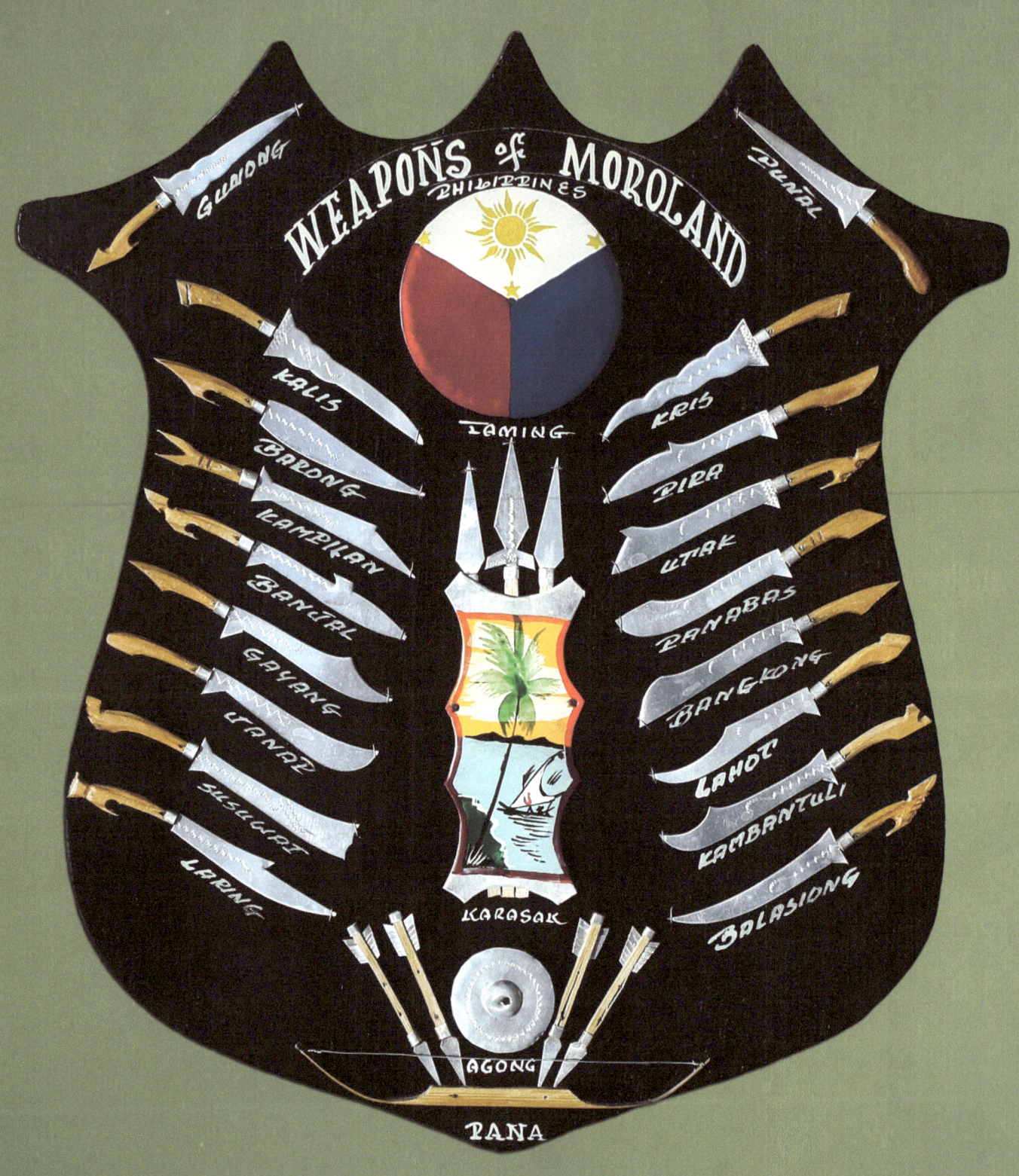

Plaque: #24 Philippines Moro Weapons

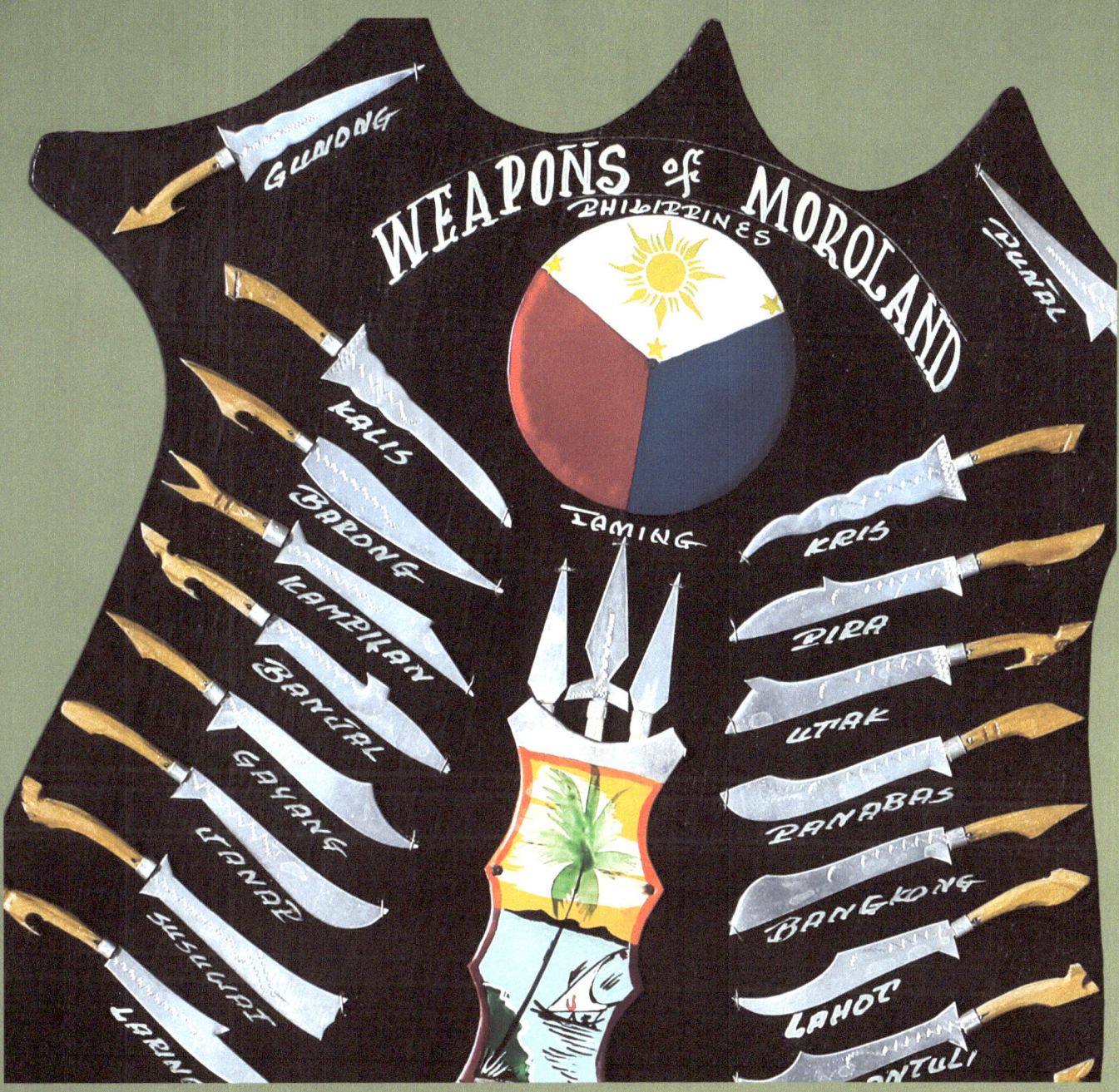

Plaque: #24 Philippines Moro Weapons

Description:

Vintage handmade Weapons Of Moroland shield. This wall display features assorted swords, arrows and other weapons.

Location Found:	Manila, Philippines	**Height:**	13 inches
Location Purchased:	EBay	**Width:**	12 inches
Approximate Age:	1960's	**Condition:**	Average

LITTLE EXTRAS

of

MOROLAND MUSEUM

BOAT PLAQUES

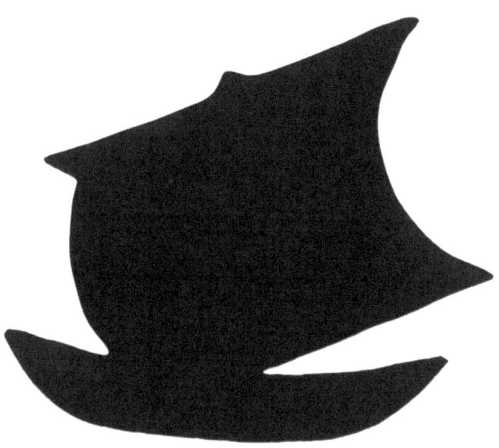

This is a special section of this book that is dedicated to the Weapons Souvenir Plaques of Moroland Museum that are shaped like a boat.
They are called Vinta (*Fishing Boat*) plaques. Three of these rare boat plaques are featured in this edition and more of these special plaques will be presented in next special edition of these souvenir plaques.

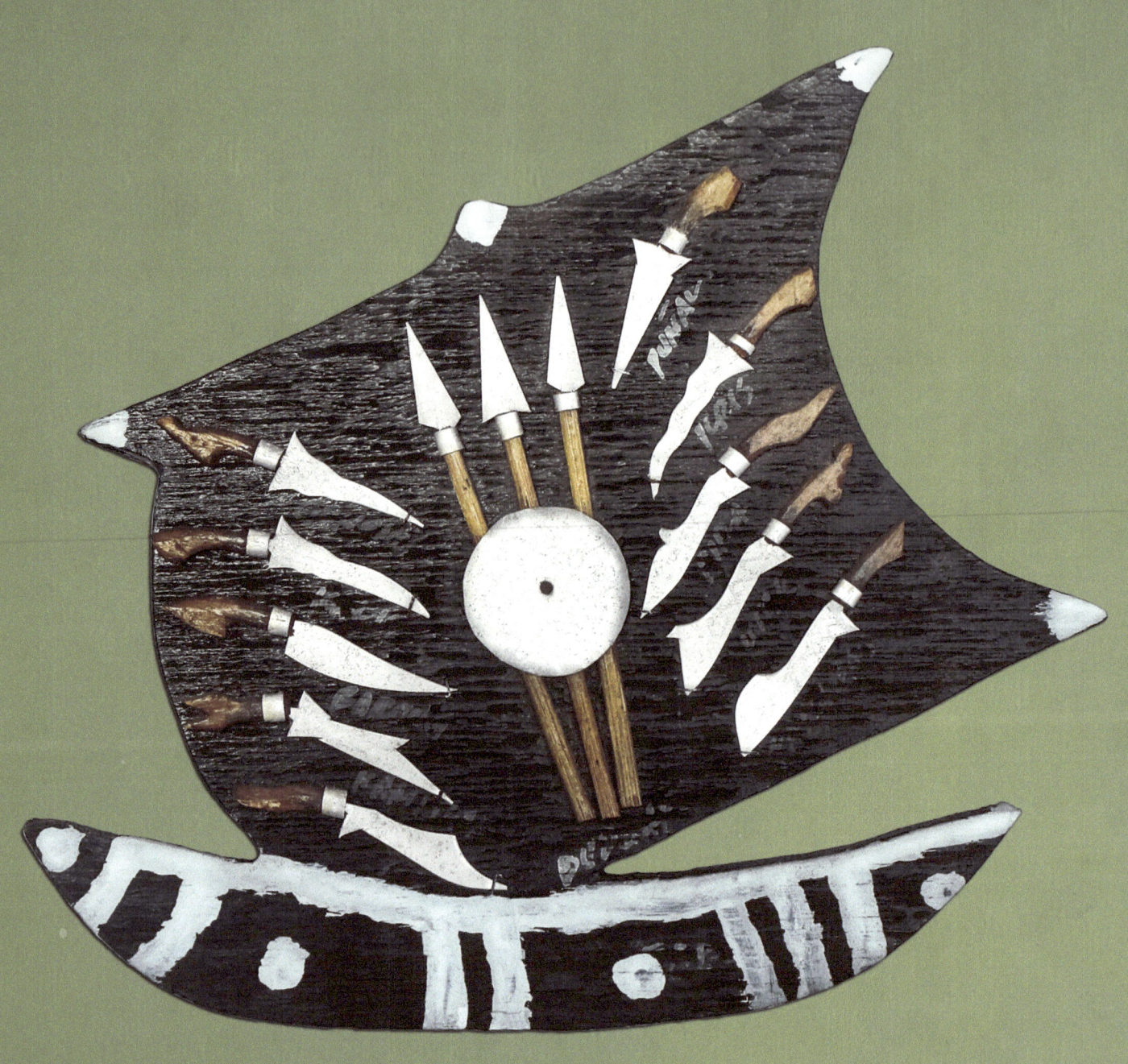

Plaque: #01 Vinta Boat Plaque

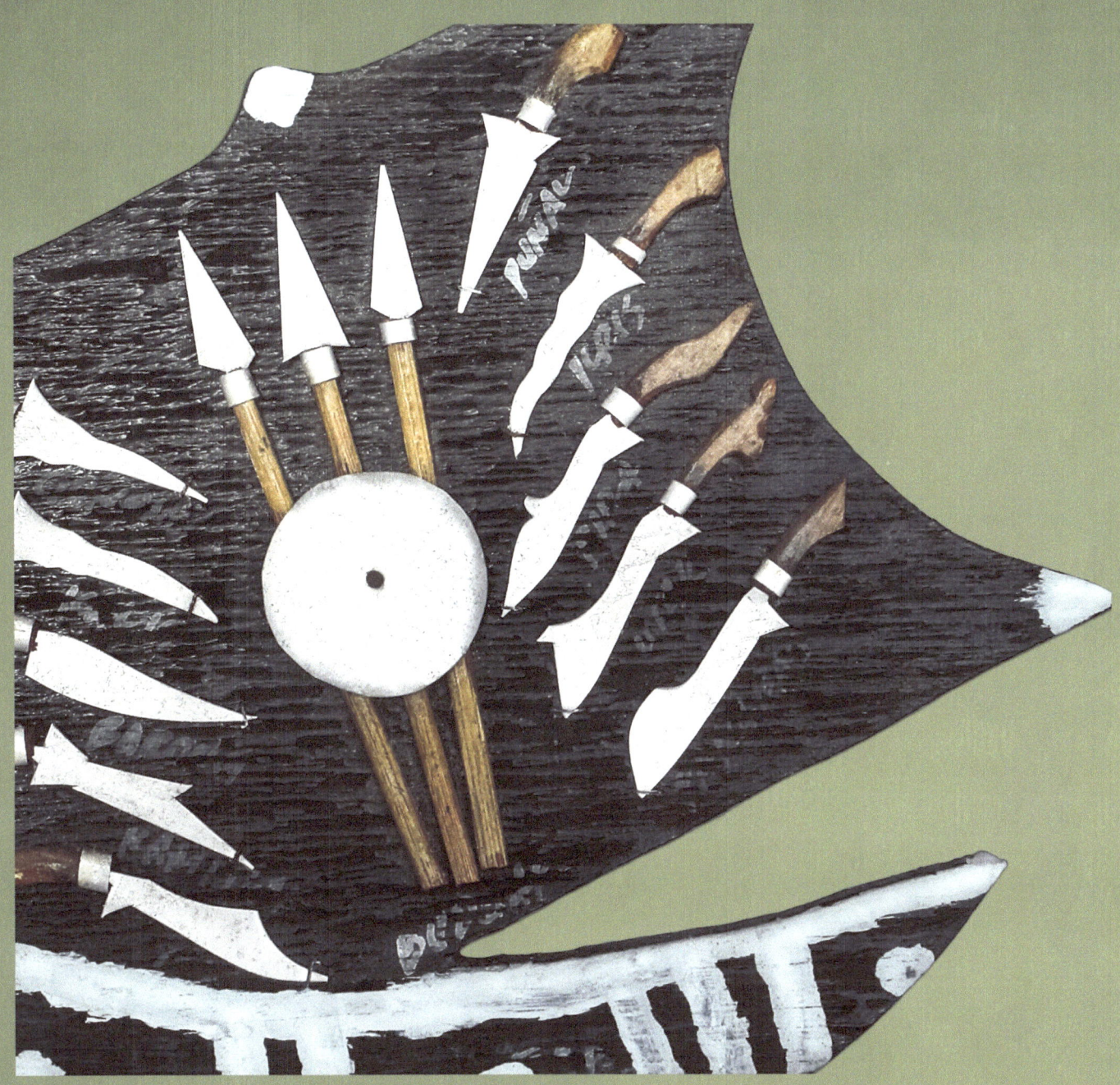

Plaque: #01 Vinta Boat Plaque

Description:

Old and Battered this rare handmade and handcarved Plaque–Weapons Of Moroland Shield. This item was brought back from the Philippines after WWII. Due to the age, most of the words are worn off.

Location Found:	Manila, Philippines	**Height:**	7 inches
Location Purchased:	EBay	**Width:**	7.5 inches
Approximate Age:	1940's	**Condition:**	Average

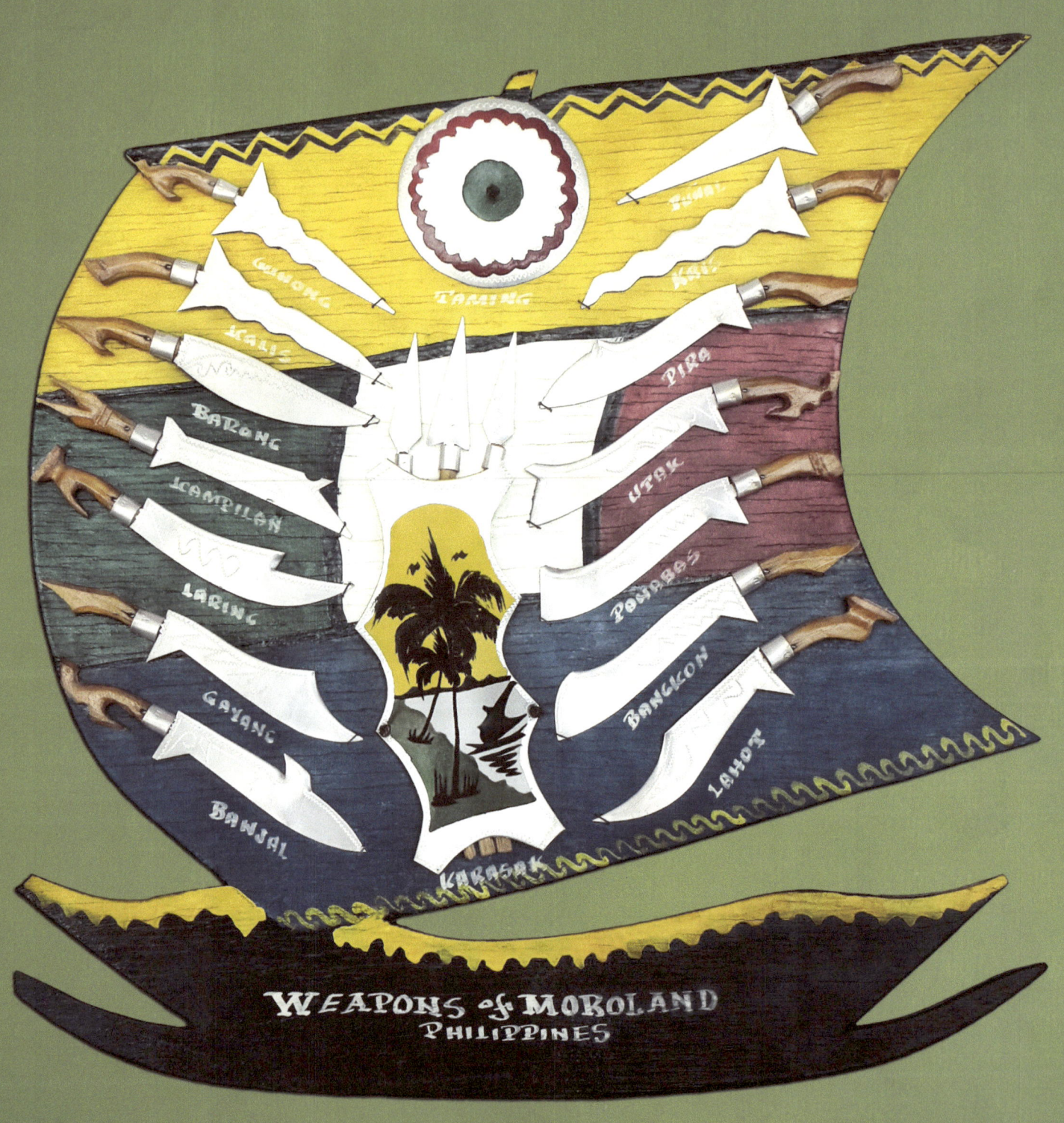

Plaque: #02 Vinta Boat Plaque

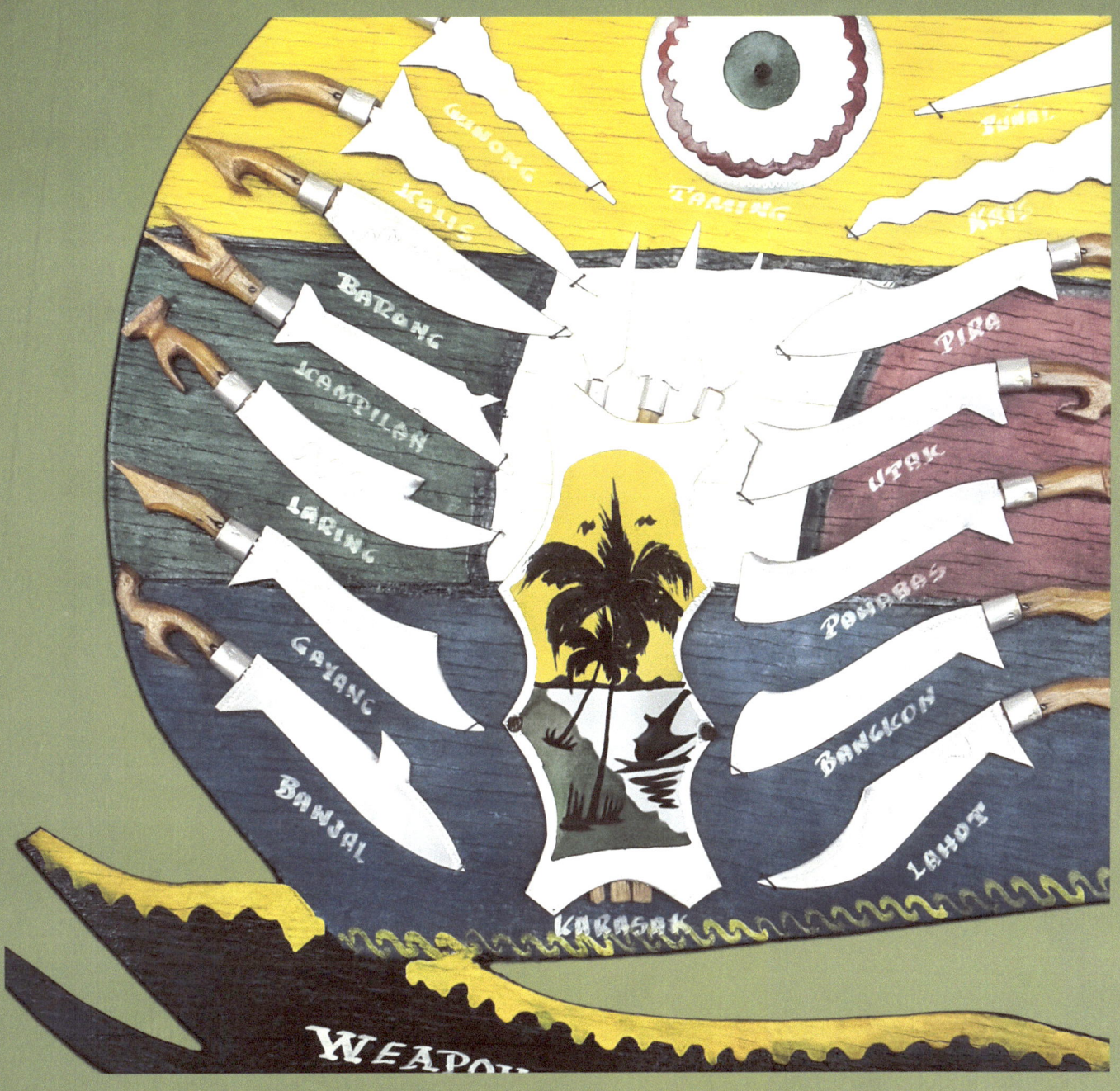

Plaque: #02 Vinta Boat Plaque

Description:

    This vintage plaque shows minature hand crafted weapons with wooden handles and tin blades. The Moro weapons displayed on this plaque are 14 daggers, 3 spears and two shields.

Location Found:	Manila, Philippines	**Height:**	9 inches
Location Purchased:	EBay	**Width:**	9 inches
Approximate Age:	1950's-60's	**Condition:**	Average

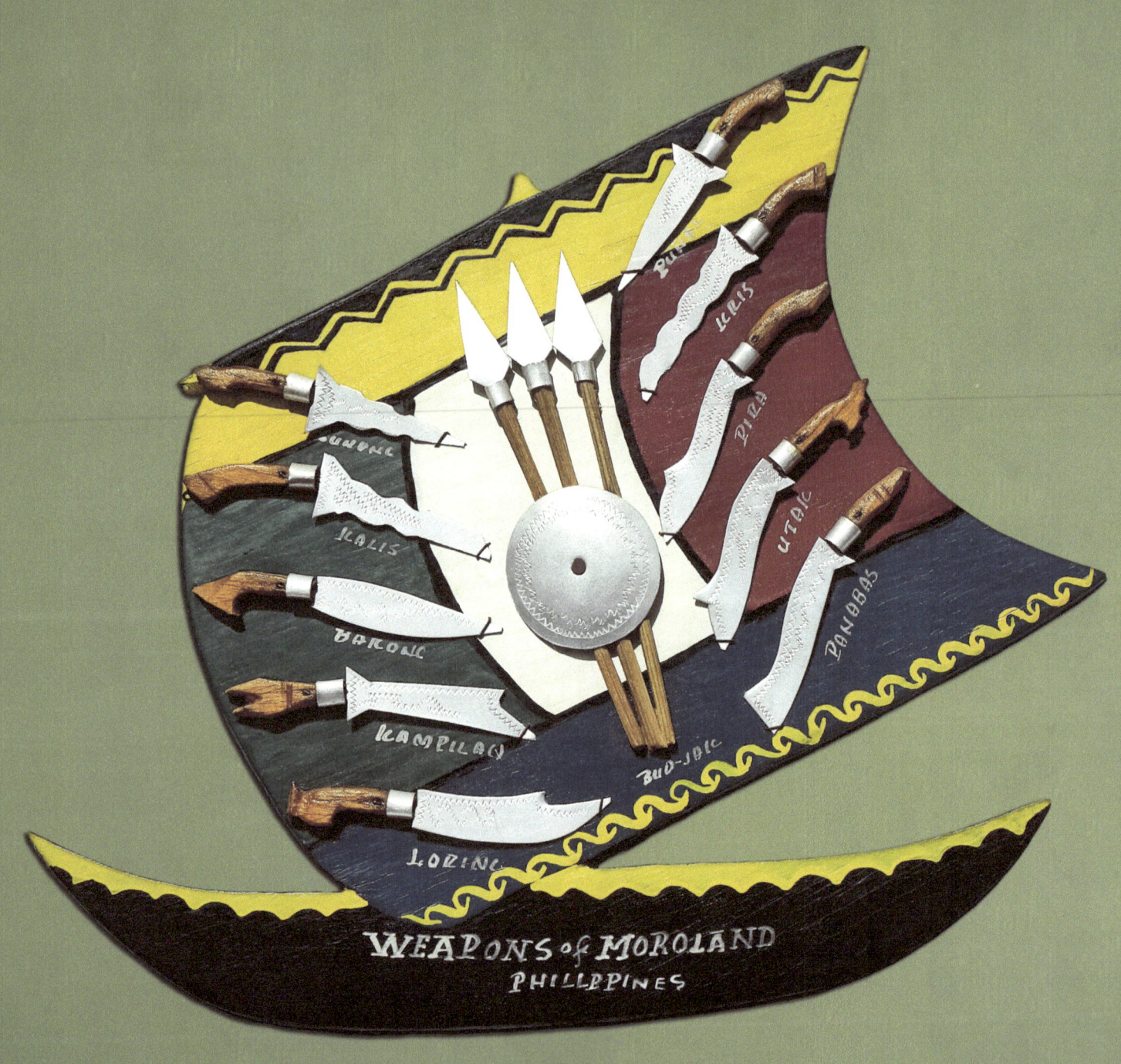

Plaque: #03 Vinta Boat Plaque

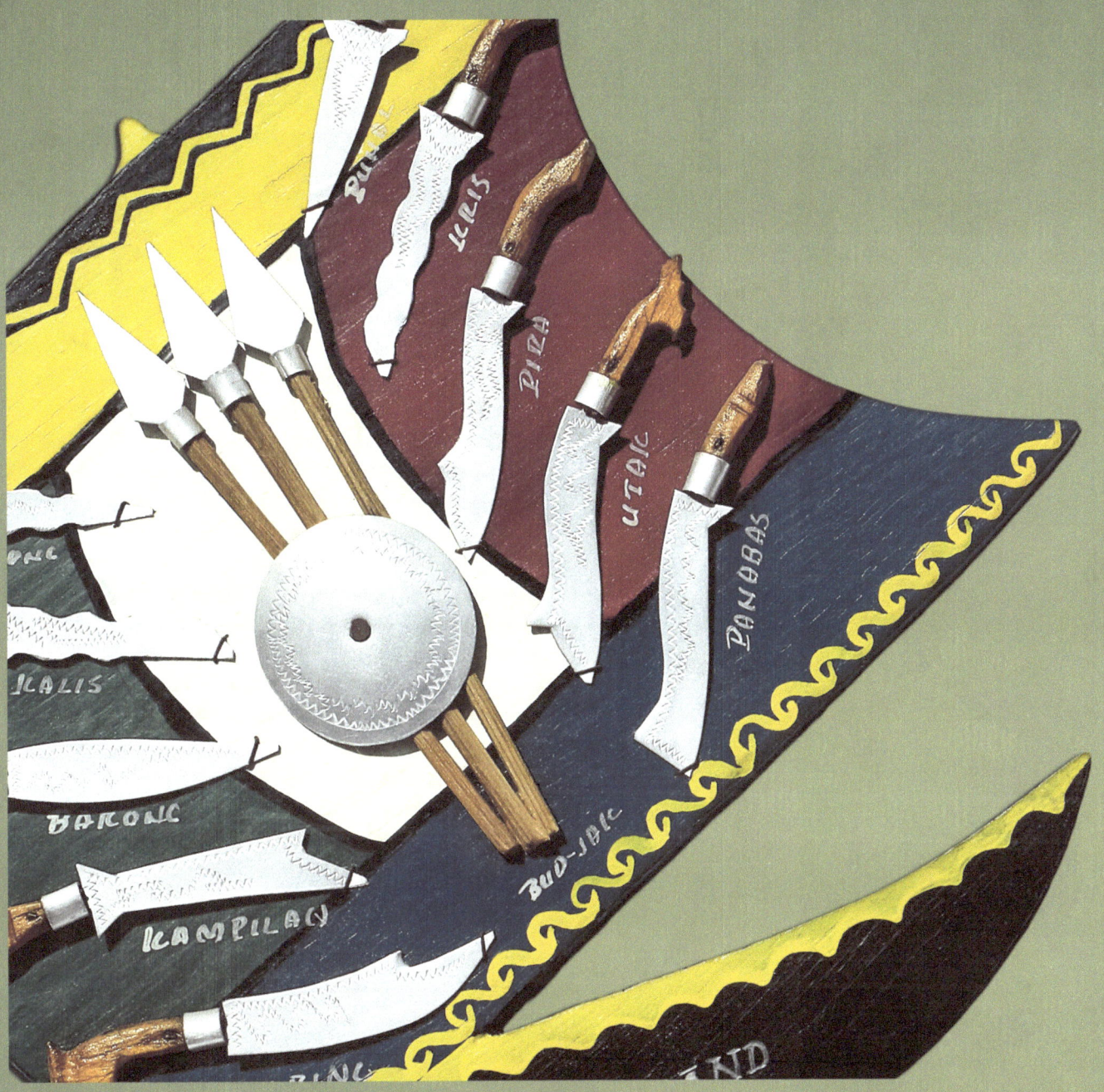

Plaque: #03 Vinta Boat Plaque

Description:

Vintage "Weapons Of Moroland" Philippines on the sail of a boat. Looks like ten knives, three spears and a shield. The knives have wooden handles and looks like aluminum blades along with the spear heads and shield. The knives are up to 2 inches long with some a little over.

Location Found:	Manila, Philippines	**Height:**	7 inches
Location Purchased:	EBay	**Width:**	7 inches
Approximate Age:	1960's	**Condition:**	Average

CONCLUSION

We hope this field guide of "Weapon Souvenir Plaques of Moroland Museum" is a helpful tool for you to use when you are hunting for your next big find or as an asset to your collection for visual reference purposes.

This guide is the first volume in a set of volumes that Moroland Historical Publications will publish on the Moroland Museum's souvenir plaques collection. The second volume will display more unique plaques (not shown in the first volume) as well as more examples of the rare Vinta Boat plaques. These souvenir plaques are a unique part of Filipino craftsmanship and cultural history. The Moroland Historical Publications team is dedicated to preserving this history by publishing guides which document these artifacts for all to see and learn from. This is the largest collections of these plaques (that we know of) and is most likely the very first time they have ever been displayed in this format to the public.

We hope you have enjoyed viewing this guide as much as our team has enjoyed creating it.

STATEMENTS

The writers of this book intentions were not to claim
to be or imply in any way that they are experts
or any kind of authority of Moroland
history, art, language, or weapons, or of
Philippine history, art, language, or weapons, or
of any other countries history, art, language, or
weapons. All of the weapons sizes and composition
were an estimated guess at the time of printing.

All items are shown "as is". MOROLAND MUSEUM will
not make any representation of warranty,
expressed or implied, as to the marketability,
fitness or condition of the items shown or
described or as to the correctness of
description, genuineness, attribution,
size, provenance, location of origination,
or period of the shown items.

The writers would like to say

THANK YOU

to those whose support and input
made this book possible.

Our Spouses, Our Children, Our Friends
We would also like to thank those curious
collectors who before us have preserved
this part of our past and those whose
skills, patience, and imagination made these
items to begin with.

IGOROT SHIELDS

of

MOROLAND MUSEUM

field guide   *fifth edition*

Igorot Shields of Moroland fifth edition has a variety of warrior shields to tempt you.

This pictorial field guide will be a valuable asset to use when you hunt for an addition to your collection or if you are simply curious. It will have a similar style of descriptions and lots of full color pages as the last issue. It has the wonderful Moroland extras that you like so much. This edition will have a variety of shields that are very similar in shape, but different in their size, appearance and design characteristics.

In the next issue you will discover what other Moroland Museum historical artifacts await your viewing pleasure.

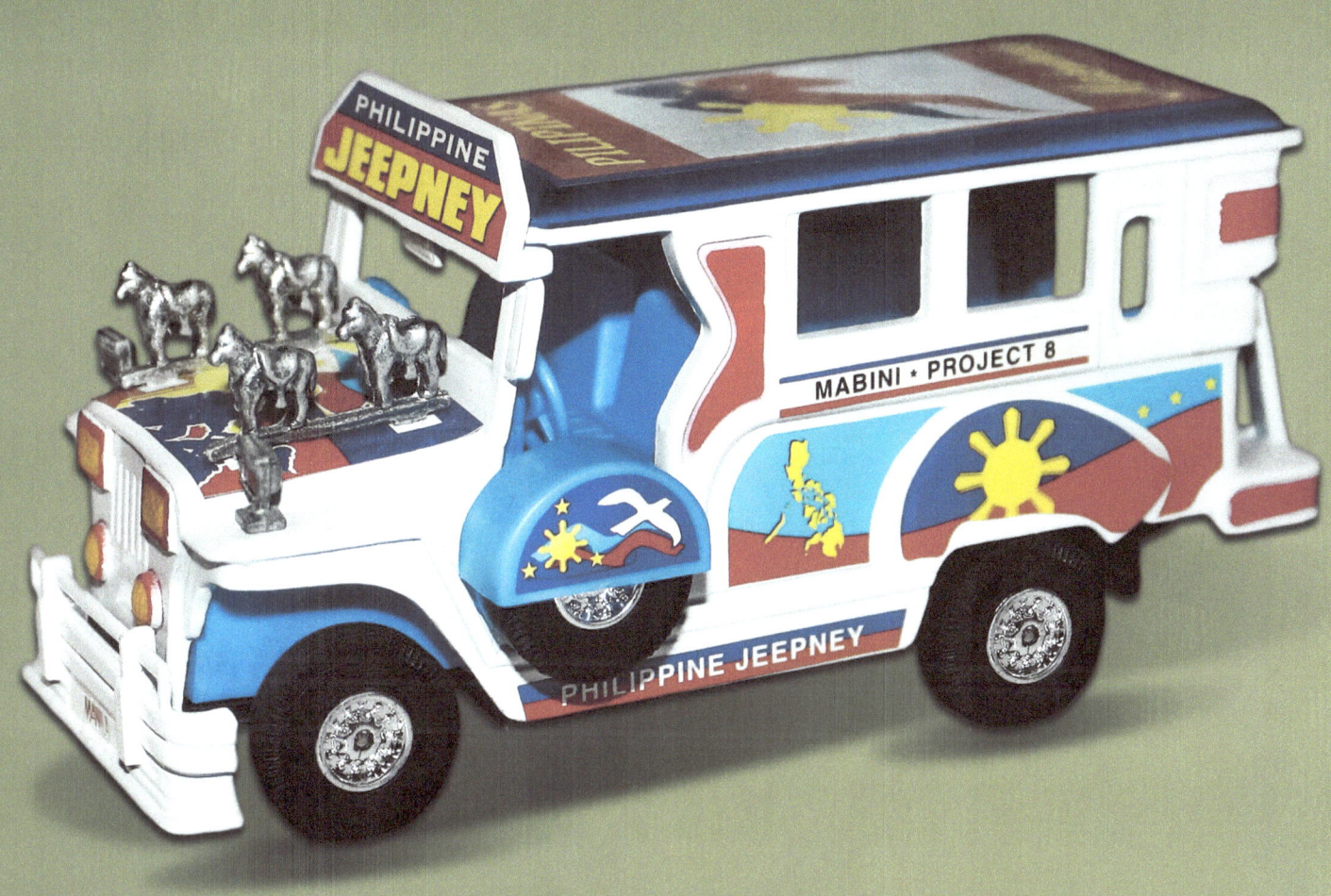

A Metal Jeepney friction toy from Makati City, Philippines. Brought back by tourist, this toy was made in 1993.

Filipino (Tagalog) Language travel phrases for Jeepney or Bus:

Please take me to (this address).	Pakihatid mo ako sa (adres na ito).
Is this the jeepney to...?	Ito ba ang dyipni na papunta sa..?
How long will it be delayed?	Gaano katagal ito maaatraso?
Is this seat free?	May nakaupo ba dito?
Please stop here.	Sa tabi lang ho.
How much is it?	Magkano?

Moroland Museum Historical Publications Book Series:

Kerises of Moroland Museum..........Book #1 on the unique Kerises (wavy blade swords) from the Moroland Museum Historical Archives, Volume #1.

Weapons of Moroland Museum.......Book #2 on the unique Weapons from the Moroland Museum Historical Archives, Volume #1.

Artifacts of Moroland Museum.........Book #3 on the unique Artifacts from the Moroland Museum Historical Archives, Volume #1.

All Moroland Museum books are available for purchase on the Amazon website and can be purchased with discount when buying in bulk.